INTELLECTUAL PROPERTY RIGHTS IN SOUND RECORDINGS, FILM & VIDEO

PROTECTION OF PHONOGRAPHIC
AND CINEMATOGRAPHIC RECORDINGS
AND WORKS
IN NATIONAL AND
INTERNATIONAL LAW

FIRST SUPPLEMENT (1994)

by

J. A. L. STERLING LL.B.
of the Middle Temple, Barrister
Senior Visiting Fellow, Queen Mary and Westfield College
University of London.

London
Sweet and Maxwell
1994

Published in 1994 by
Sweet and Maxwell Limited of
South Quay Plaza, 183 Marsh Wall,
London E14 9FT
Typeset by York House Typographic Ltd.,
London W13 8NT
Printed in Great Britain by
The Headway Press Ltd.

No natural forests were destroyed to make this product:
only farmed timber was used and re-planted

**A CIP catalogue record for this book is
available from the British Library**

ISBN Main Work 0 421 45470 9
Supplement 0 421 50420 X

All rights reserved.
UK Statutory material in this publication
is acknowledged as Crown copyright

The author has in respect of this work asserted generally
his right of identification under section 77 of the U.K.
Copyright, Designs and Patents Act 1988

*No part of this publication may be reproduced or transmitted
in any form or by any means, or stored in any retrieval system of
any nature without prior written permission of the copyright holder
and the publisher, except as specifically permitted by law, or in
accordance with the terms of a licence issued by the Copyright
Licensing Agency in respect of photocopying and/or reprographic
reproduction. Application for permission for other use of copyright
material including permission to reproduce extracts in other
published works shall be made to the publisher.*

©
J.A.L. STERLING
1994

ACKNOWLEDGEMENTS

I thank the following for provision of information or material included in the Supplement: the World Intellectual Property Organisation; the E.C. Commission; the Council of Europe; the Intellectual Property Policy Directorate of the United Kingdom Patent Office; the Intellectual Property Law Unit, Centre for Commercial Law Studies, Queen Mary and Westfield College, University of London; Elisabeth Iles, Manager, and Jacqueline Smith, Senior Information Assistant, of the Library and Information Services of the IFPI Secretariat; Freyke Bus, Trevor M. Cook, Mary Footer, Dr. Ysolde Gendreau, Ilse Hendrix, Yousef Khalilieh, Makeen Fouad Makeen, Ksenia Orlova, George Paravantis, Professor Heiki Pisuke, Igor Pozhitkov, Qiu Anman, Dr. Nicholas Rouart and Bankole Sodipo. I also thank Brigitte Lindner, Legal Adviser, IFPI Secretariat, for provision of texts and translations of a number of laws, and for valuable comments. The assistance of the staff of Messrs. Sweet & Maxwell, and the help of my wife in the preparation of the text, have been invaluable.

J. A. L. Sterling

PREFACE

The main text of this work, published in 1992, was based on information available as at October 31, 1991.

The succeeding years 1992 and 1993 form a remarkable period in the history of copyright, author's right and neighbouring rights legislation. During this period, over 30 countries introduced new laws in the field, or adopted substantial amendments to existing legislation, often introducing new rights and increasing penalties for infringement. A number of countries joined the Berne Convention, the U.C.C., the Rome Convention, or the Phonograms Convention. Three Directives of the European Community (on rental and lending rights and neighbouring rights, satellite and cable retransmission and duration of protection) will markedly affect the laws of the Member States. Other important developments include the adoption of the GATT Agreement, with its TRIPs Agreement annex, and meetings to discuss new international instruments concerning the Berne Convention, and the rights of performers and phonogram producers.

Some of the factors which may be considered as causing or contributing to these developments are the following:

(1) *The general increase in the value of intellectual property rights.*

(2) *The fruition of the work carried out over a number of years by the World Intellectual Property Organisation (WIPO)* in promoting studies in and training sessions in relation to the techniques of legislating on and administering intellectual property rights. WIPO's activities in this direction do not always receive extensive publicity, but some idea as to their extent can be gained from the reports appearing in *Copyright*: these cover the activities of WIPO in relation to developing countries and European countries in transmission to market economies, as well as numerous contacts with Governments and international organisations.

(3) *The expansion of cable and satellite services, and their increased use of film and video,* requiring new methods of clearance of the intellectual property rights involved.

(4) *The realisation by major exporters of intellectual property, particularly the United States, of the importance of ensuring world wide recognition of intellectual property exploitation rights*, and the consequent economic pressure brought to bear on countries which are considered as not reaching the required standards of protection.

(5) *The influence of the acceptance by the super-powers of high level protection of copyright and author's right*, witnessed by the effects of the accession by the United States to the Berne Convention (1989), China's membership of the Berne Convention (1992) and the Russian Federation's adoption of an author's right law recognising the basic approaches of the Berne and Rome 1961 Conventions.

(6) *The influence of campaigns undertaken by such international organisations as IFPI*, aimed at achieving establishment and recognition of the relevant rights at the highest level, particularly in relation to measures for the prevention of piracy.

(7) *International developments affecting economic relations between States*, particularly in the context of GATT, the European Union, the North American Free Trade Agreement (NAFTA) and the Asian Pacific Economic Cooperation forum (APEC), in all of which the importance of effective implementation of intellectual property rights has been or will undoubtedly be recognised.

(8) *The introduction of new legislation following the break-up of the U.S.S.R. and Yugoslavia.*

Updating of main text

In order to give an overview of this activity, a Summary of Developments is given hereunder, followed in the main body of the Supplement by descriptions of the various new laws and developments under the respective paragraph numbers of the main text.

A general note on the current position in the Republics of the former U.S.S.R. and the successor States of Yugoslavia will be found in paragraph 21.01. The recent developments and changed legal situations result in new entries in the Synopsis of Laws for Estonia, Latvia, Lithuania, Armenia, Azerbaidjan, Belarus, Georgia, Kazakhstan, Kirghizia, Moldova, Russian Federation, Tadjikistan, Turkmenistan, Ukraine and Uzbekistan as regards former U.S.S.R., and Bosnia-Herzegovina, Croatia, Macedonia, Montenegro, Serbia and Slovenia as regards former Yugoslavia. There are also

Preface

new synopsis entries for the Czech Republic (para. 27.70) and the Slovak Republic (para. 42.65).

Where the text or a translation of a new law has been available, the corresponding entries in paragraphs 7.46 (Rome Convention: sharing of equitable remuneration), 7B.21 (level of performer's protection), 7B.22 (duration of performer's protection), 7B.23 (performer's share of private copying payments), 7C.02 *et seq.* (performer's and producer's protection), 20.22 (List I: levels of protection), 20.25 (List II: duration of protection), 20.28 (List III: recording machine and tape payments), 20.31 (List IV: rental), and 20.51 (Chart), are listed under the respective paragraph numbers (and in the Index of Countries and Territories) to reflect the respective Synopsis entry. Where, however, such a text or translation has not been available, the report is limited to the Synopsis entry.

Reference to paragraph numbers

References to paragraph numbers are, unless otherwise specified, to paragraphs of this Supplement. References to paragraphs of the main text are indicated by 'main text' before the paragraph number.

'Sound works'

With reference to the first paragraph of the main text preface it may be noted that 'sound works' (distinguishing goods or services) may be registered as trade marks in certain jurisdictions, including Canada and the United States (see *WIPR* 1991, May, 323).

Status juris

The Supplement is based on material available as at January 1, 1994, including the January 1994 issue of *Copyright*. It has been possible in some cases to include material which has become available after that date, and to give a summary of the Council of Europe Convention on Transfrontier Satellite Broadcasting, February 16, 1994 (see para. 7.50).

Belgium

A Bill completely modernising the law on author's right and neighbouring rights is proceeding through the Belgian Parliament. The definitive provisions of the Law remain to be finalised, but according to the version of the

Bill of March 1994, authors are granted Level I(m) protection (70 years p.m.a.), performers are granted Level Ix(m) protection (50 years), and phonogram producers and film first fixation producers are granted Level Ix and Level I protection respectively (50 years). Rental rights are granted to authors, performers, phonogram producers and film first fixation producers. The Bill's provisions on a system of remuneration for private copying (for the benefit of authors, performers and producers and certain other participants) are still under discussion.

Egypt

By virtue of the Prime Ministerial Decree of April 28, 1994, sound recordings are considered audio works subject to protection under Law No. 354 of 1954. In addition, the Decree defines financial exploitation of a work in terms of articles 5 and 6 of the 1954 Law (such exploitation to be carried out only by or with the written consent of the author or his successor) as the following: rental, and the rights to authorise copying, public performance, broadcasting and cabling. From this information, it is understood that sound recordings now enjoy Level I(m) protection in Egypt, with a protection period of 50 years p.m.a.

Estonia

Estonia's accession to the Paris text 1971 of the Berne Convention has been approved by the Law passed by the Estonian Parliament on May 18, 1994.

Hungary

By the 1994 amending Law (entering into force on July 1, 1994), Law No. III of 1969 is amended in a number of important respects, including the following.

The author's economic rights are protected for life plus 70 years p.m.a. The term of protection for films is extended to 70 years after the year of showing. Protection for performers is provided in a formulation close to that of Article 7 of the Rome Convention 1961 (with the limitation as provided in Art. 19 of the Convention). The phonogram producer is granted the rights of authorising reproduction, distribution and importation of the phonogram; the phonogram producer also has the right to have his name indicated on copies of the phonogram. A right to remuneration in respect of the use of commercially published phonograms for broadcasting or any other communication to the public is introduced for the benefit of performers and phonogram producers. Rights are granted to authors, performers and phonogram producers in respect of the public lending or rental of copies of phonograms distributed to the public. A remuneration right in respect of private copying is introduced for the benefit of authors, performers and producers, payable by manufacturers and importers of sound and video carriers. The period of protection for performances and phonograms is 50 years.

Poland

The new Law on author's right and neighbouring rights (which entered into effect on May 23, 1994) increases the general standard of protection for authors, and introduces comprehensive provisions on neighbouring rights, providing Level I(m) protection for authors (50 years p.m.a. (50 years in the case of audiovisual works, economic rights vesting in the producer)), Level Ix(m) protection for performers (50 years) and Level Ix protection for producers of phonograms and videograms (50 years). Authors, performers and phonogram and videogram producers are granted specific rental and lending rights. Private copying remuneration rights are instituted for the benefit of authors, performers and producers of audio and video recordings, manufacturers and importers of recording equipment and blank carriers being obliged to make payments at the rate provided by law.

Producers and publishers of public domain works published in Poland are obliged to make payments (five to eight per cent. of gross receipts from sale of copies of these works) to the Fund for the Promotion of Creativity. (*C.f.* para. 8.34 of the main text.) Extensive civil and criminal remedies are instituted.

The availability of the English translation by Bianka A. Kortlan of the text of the 1994 Law is gratefullly acknowledged.

Ukraine

It is reported that the new author's right and neighbouring rights law of the Ukraine entered into effect on February 23, 1994, and that authors of works are granted protection for the author's life plus 50 years; performers and recording producers also receive protection. See *WIPR* 1994, April, 10.

Lamb Chambers, Lamb Building, The Temple, London EC4Y 7AS	J. A. L. Sterling June 1, 1994

TABLE OF CONTENTS

	page
Acknowledgements	iii
Preface	v
Summary of developments	xiii
Table of Cases	xxiii
Table of International Treaties and Conventions	xxvii
Table of European Materials	xxix
Table of Legislative Instruments	xxxi
Supplement notes to Part I	1
Supplement notes to Part II	49
Bibliography	173
Index of Countries and Territories	177
General Index	185

SUMMARY OF DEVELOPMENTS

The following is a summary of developments of which notice has been received since October 31, 1991 (the date of the *status juris* of the main text) up to January 1, 1994 (or, in some instances, a later date, as indicated). Additional details will be found in the Supplement paragraphs indicated. Developments in other areas, details of other laws, decrees and regulations published in *Copyright* from November 1991 to January 1994 inclusive, new cases, etc., are listed in the Supplement under the applicable main text paragraph numbers. Among new cases, mention may be made of the important decision of the European Court of Justice in *Phil Collins* (see para. 7.38).

A general note on the current position in the Republics of the former U.S.S.R. and the successor States of Yugoslavia will be found in paragraph 21.01. As to the Czech Republic and the Slovak Republic, see paragraphs 27.70 and 42.65 respectively.

A. Membership of Conventions, Treaties and Agreements

The following countries have become members (or, in the case of succession, confirmed their membership) of the Conventions, Treaties and Agreements as indicated:

I. *Conventions*

(1) **Berne Convention**:

Albania, Bolivia, Bosnia-Herzegovina, China, Croatia, Czech Republic, El Salvador, Gambia, Jamaica, Kenya, Macedonia, Namibia, Nigeria, St. Lucia, Slovak Republic, Slovenia. (Switzerland (already a member) has ratified the Paris text 1971 of the Convention.)

[*Post* January 1, 1994: Tanzania.]

(2) **Universal Copyright Convention:**
Bosnia-Herzegovina, China, Croatia, Czech Republic, Kazakhstan, Russian Federation, Slovak Republic, Slovenia, Tadjikistan, Uruguay. (Switzerland (already a member) has ratified the Paris text 1971 of the Convention.)

(3) **Rome Convention 1961:**
Argentina, Australia, Bolivia, Czech Republic, Greece, Jamaica, Netherlands, Nigeria, Slovak Republic, Switzerland.

(4) **Phonograms Convention 1971:**
China, Cyprus, Czech Republic, Greece, Jamaica, Netherlands, Slovak Republic, Switzerland.

[*Post* January 1, 1994: Colombia.]

(5) **WIPO Convention:**
Albania, Armenia, Bhutan, Bolivia, Bosnia-Herzegovina, Croatia, Czech Republic, Estonia, Kazakhstan, Latvia, Lithuania, Macedonia, Moldova, Russian Federation, St. Lucia, Slovak Republic, Slovenia, Uzbekistan.

[*Post* January 1, 1994: Brunei Darussalam, Georgia, Kyrgyz Republic, Tajikistan.]

(6) **Satellites Convention 1974:**
Armenia, Croatia, Greece, Russian Federation, Slovenia, Switzerland.
See paragraphs 20.11, 20.12.

[*Post* January 1, 1994: Council of Europe Transfrontier Satellite Broadcasting Convention 1994: see paragraph 7.51.]

II. *Treaty*

Treaty on the International Registration of Audiovisual Works:
Argentina, Brazil, Chile, Czech Republic, Slovak Republic.
See paragraph 7.49.

[*Post* January 1, 1994: Colombia, Peru, Senegal.]

B. Laws, Decrees and Regulations

Albania

—Law No. 7564 of May 19, 1992 (rights of authors, performers, etc.).
See paragraph 21.20.

Angola

—Law on Author's Rights, No. 4/90 of March 10, 1990 (protection of author's right).
See paragraph 21.60.

Australia

—Copyright Amendment Act, 1993 (importation of books).
See paragraph 22.30.

Austria

—Amending Law UrhGNov 1993, of February 11 1993 (rental).
See paragraph 22.60.

Bahrain

—Decree No. 10/1993, Official Gazette, No. 2039 of June 9, 1993.
See paragraph 22.95.

Bolivia

—Law 1322 of April 13, 1992 (protection of performers, phonogram producers and broadcasting organisations).
See paragraph 23.80.

Bulgaria

—Law of June 16, 1993 (author's right and neighbouring rights).
See paragraph 24.70.

Canada

—Copyright Act amendments 1990, 1992, 1993.
See paragraph 25.30.

Chile

—Amendment Law No. 19.166 of September 9, 1992 (duration, rights of phonogram producers).
See paragraph 25.90.

China

—International Copyright Treaties Implementating Rules, September 25, 1992.
—Regulations for Protection of Computer Software.
See paragraph 26.00

Colombia

—Amending Law, No. 44 of February 5, 1993 (duration of protection, remedies and penalties).
See paragraph 26.50.

Cyprus

—Copyright (Amendment) Law 1993 (duration, importation rights, penalties).
See paragraph 25.70.

Denmark

—Amending Law, No. 338 of May 14, 1992 (blank tape payment).
See paragraph 27.80.

Ecuador

—Amending Law, No. 161 of July 14, 1992 (criminal penalties and civil remedies concerning unauthorised reproduction, sale, etc.).
See paragraph 28.30.

Egypt

—Amending Law No. 38 of June 4, 1992 (protection of authors, etc.).
—Implementing Regulations, Ministerial Decree No. 162/1993.
See paragraph 28.40.

SUMMARY OF DEVELOPMENTS

El Salvador

—Decree 604 of July 15, 1993 (author's right and neighbouring rights).
See paragraph 28.50.

Estonia

—Law of November 11, 1992 (protection of authors, performers, phonogram producers and broadcasting organisations).
See paragraph 28.60.

Finland

—Amending Law, No. 34 of January 11, 1991 (rights of authors, performers and phonogram producers).
See paragraph 29.20.

France

—Code of July 1, 1992, as amended to December 16, 1992 (consolidating and amending previous law).
See paragraph 29.30.

Germany

—Amending Law of June 9, 1993 (computer programs).
See paragraph 30.20.

Greece

—Law of March 3, 1993 (author's right and related rights).
See paragraph 30.50.

Honduras

—Decree No. 131–91 of October 31, 1991 (criminal penalties and phonogram producers' rights concerning unauthorised reproduction of phonograms).
See paragraph 31.70.

Hungary

—Penal Code, amendment of March 2, 1993 (increase of penalties for infringement).
See paragraph 31.90.

Iceland

—Amending Law of May 19, 1992 (rights of performers and phonogram producers).
See paragraph 32.10.

India

—Copyright Amendment Ordinance, No. 9 of 1991 (duration of copyright in works, sound recordings, films, etc.).
See paragraph 32.20.

Isle of Man

—Copyright Act 1991.
See paragraph 32.70.

Italy

—Law No. 93 of February 5, 1992 (blank tape payment and administration of performers' rights).
See paragraph 32.90.

Jamaica

—Copyright Act 1993.
See paragraph 33.10.

Japan

—Amending Law, No. 106 of December 16, 1992 (blank tape payments).
See paragraph 33.20.

SUMMARY OF DEVELOPMENTS

Jordan

—Law No. 22 of 1992 (protection of authors and performers).
See paragraph 33.30.

Latvia

—Law of May 11, 1993 (author's right and neighbouring rights).
See paragraph 34.35.

Malta

—Copyright Amendment Act 1992 (criminal penalties for copyright infringement).
See paragraph 36.00.

Netherlands

—Law on Neighbouring Rights of March 18, 1993.
See paragraph 37.70.

Niger

—Ordinance on the Protection of Copyright, Neighbouring Rights and Expressions of Folklore, No. 93/93.
See paragraph 38.40.

Nigeria

—Copyright Amendment Decree No. 98, 1992 (blank tape payments).
See paragraph 38.50.

Norway

—Amending Law of June 9, 1993.
See paragraph 38.90.

Poland

[—*Post* January 1, 1994: Law of February 4, 1994 on Author's Right and Neighbouring Rights.
See paragraph 40.30.]

Russian Federation

—Resolution of the Supreme Soviet of the Russian Federation governing Civil Legal Relations arising during the Implementation of the Economic Reform No. 3301–1 of July 14, 1992.
—Law on Author's Right and Neighbouring Rights 1993 (protection of authors, performers, phonogram producers and broadcasting organisations).
See paragraph 41.10.

St. Vincent and the Grenadines

—Copyright Act 1989.
See paragraph 41.80.

San Marino

—Law of January 25, 1991 (author's and performer's rights).
See paragraph 42.00.

Saudi Arabia

—Regulations on deposit of copyright applications, Royal Decree M/26 of March 11, 1992.
See paragraph 42.20.

Spain

—Amending Law 20/1992 of July 7, 1992 (blank tape payments, etc.).
—Decree No. 1434/92 of November 27, 1992 (blank tape payments, etc.).
See paragraph 43.00.

Sweden

—Act No. 1685 of 1992 (computer programs and semiconductor chip protection).
See paragraph 43.60.

Switzerland

—Law of October 9, 1992 (author's right and rights of performers, phonogram producers and broadcasting organisations).
See paragraph 43.70.

Summary of Developments

Taiwan

—Law of June 10, 1992, as amended by Laws of July 6, 1992 and April 24, 1993 (protection of literary, artistic etc. works, including sound recordings and audiovisual works).
See paragraph 44.00.

Togo

—Law No. 91–12 of June 10, 1991 (protection of authors, performers, phonogram producers and broadcasting organisations).
See paragraph 44.30.

United Arab Emirates

—Federal Law No. 40 of September 28, 1992 (protection of authors).
See paragraph 45.60.

United States of America

—Audio Home Recording Act 1992 (blank digital tape payments and technical control devices).
See paragraph 45.90.

Venezuela

—Law of August 14, 1993 (protection of author's rights and neighbouring rights).
See paragraph 46.60.

C. European Community Directives

Council Directive 92/100 on rental and lending rights, and related rights;
Council Directive 93/83 on satellite broadcasting and cable retransmission;
Council Directive 93/93 on term of protection.
See paragraph 7.51.

D. Other International Instruments

Possible Protocol to the Berne Convention. See paragraph 7.50.
Possible Instrument on the Protection of the Rights of Performers and Producers of Phonograms. See paragraph 7.50.

GATT-TRIPs Agreement (December 15, 1993). See paragraph 7.52.
European Economic Area Agreement. See paragraph 7.54.
North American Free Trade Agreement. See paragraph 7.55.

TABLE OF CASES

Austria

"Direct Satellite Broadcasting II" (OLG Vienna, June 27, 1991) *GRUR Int.* 1991, 925... 7.26
"Direct Satellite Broadcasting III" (OGH, June 16, 1992) *IIC* 1993, 665...... 7.26

Australia

Australian Tape Manufacturers Assn. Ltd and ors v. Commonwealth of Australia (1993) 176 C.L.R. 480, 112 A.L.R. 53 (High Court) 22.30
Autodesk Inc. and anor v. Dyason and ors [1992] R.P.C. 575, (1992) 172 C.L.R. 330, 22 I.P.R. 163, 104 A.L.R. 563 (High Court, rehearing refused [1993] R.P.C. 259, 25 I.P.R. 33, (1993) 111 A.L.R. 385)................. 4.25

Canada

Canadian Admiral Corp. Ltd. v. Rediffusion Inc. (1954) 20 C.P.R. 75, [1954] Ex. C.R. 382.. 25.30, 45.70
Canadian Cable Television Association v. Copyright Board et al. 46 C.P.R. 359 (Fed. Ct. of Appeal 1993)...................................... 25.30
CAPAC v. CTV Television Network Ltd. [1968] S.C.R. 676, (1968) 55 C.P.R. (2d) 132. .... 25.30
Delrina Corp. v. Triolet Systems Inc. (1993) 47 C.P.R. (3d) 1 (Ontario Ct., Gen. Div.) 4.25
Performing Rights Organisation of Canada Ltd. et al v. CTV Television Network Ltd. et al. (1993) 46 C.P.R. 3d 343 (Fed. Ct. of Appeal, 1993) 25.30

Denmark

Nordisk Copyright Bureau v. Municipality of Søllerød [1994] *EIPR* D-6...... 20.31

France

Turner Entertainment Co. v. Huston et al. *RIDA* 149, 197; *IIC* 1992, 702 (Cour de Cassation) 7.15

Germany

Duo Gismonti-Vasconcelos (LG Munich, May 17, 1991) *GRUR Int.* 1993, 82 . 30.20
"Videoweitausverwertung II" *GRUR Int.* 1994, 41 (BGH, 1993) 30.20

Greece

Forgery of Videotapes (Areopagus, 1990) [1993] F.S.R. 704. . . . . 7.42

Ireland

Correction, Radio Telefis "Eireann", not "Eirann"

South Africa

Nintendo Co. Ltd. v. Golden China TV Game Centre (SC, 1993) [1994] *Ent. L.R.* E-8) 4.26

Switzerland

Elvis Presley Records *GRUR Int.* 1993, 707 (BG August 18, 1993) 43.70

United Kingdom

IBCOS Computers Ltd. v. Poole and ors. (Ch.D., Jacob J., February 24, 1994). . 4.26
John Richardson Computers Ltd. v. Flanders and anor. [1993] F.S.R. 497 (Ch.D.). 4.26
Mad Mat Husic Ltd. v. Pulse Eight Records Ltd., note in [1992] *Ent. L.R.* E-79 (Ch.D., Mervyn Davies J., 1992). 7B.16
Morrison Leahy Music Ltd. & anor. v. Lightbond Ltd. & ors. [1993] E.M.L.R. 144, summary in [1992] *Ent. L.R.* 26 (Ch.D.) 4.70
Time Warner Entertainment Co. LP v. Channel Four Television Corp. PLC and anor. [1994] E.M.L.R. 1 (C.A.). 7.41

Table of Cases

United States of America

Apple Computer Inc. v. Microsoft Corp. 779 F. Supp. 133, 20 USPQ 2d 1236 (N.D. Calif. 1991); 24 USPQ 2d 1081, 24 I.P.R. 225 (N.D. Calif. 1992); 27 USPQ 2d 1081 (N.D. Calif. 1993) 4.26
Atari Games Corp. v. Nintendo of America Inc. 24 USPQ 2d 1015 (C.A.F.C. 1992) 4.26
Autoskill Inc. v. National Education Support Systems Inc. 26 USPQ 2d 1828 (C.A. 10, 1993) 4.25
Bellsouth Advertising and Publishing Corp. v. Donnelly Information Publishing Inc. 19 USPQ 2d 1345; 28 USPQ 2d 1001 (C.A. 11, 1993) 4.24
BMG Music v. Perex 952 F. 2d 318 (C.A. 9, 1991) 45.90
Broadcast Music Inc. v. Claire's Boutiques Inc. has been affirmed: 949 F. 2d 1482; 21 USPQ 2d 118 (C.A. 7, 1991, cert. denied – USLW – 1992) 45.90
Brown Bag Software v. Symantec Corp. 960 F. 2d 1465; 22 USPQ 2d 1429 (C.A. 9, 1992 cert. denied October 5, 1992) 4.25
Coleman v. ESPN Inc. 20 USPQ 2d 1513 (S.D.N.Y. 1991) 45.90
Columbia Pictures Ind. Inc. v. Professional Real Estate Investors Inc. 944 F. 2d. 1525; 19 USPQ 2d 1771 (C.A. 9, 1991, cert. granted 112 S. Ct. 1557 (1992)) 45.90
Computer Associates International Inc. v. Altai Inc. 775 F. Supp. 544 (E.D.N.Y. 1991); 982 F. 2d 693, 23 USPQ 2d 1241 (C.A. 2, 1992) 4.25, 4.26
Edison Bros. Stores Inc. v. Broadcast Music Inc. has been affirmed: 954 F. 2d 1419; 21 USPQ 2d 1440 (C.A. 8, 1992, cert. denied – USLW – 1992) 45.90
Gates Rubber Co. v. Bands Chemical Industries Ltd. 28 USPQ 2d 1503 (C.A. 10, 1993) 4.25
Grand Upright Music Ltd. v. Warner Brothers Records Inc. et al. [1992] *Ent. L.R.* E-27 (S.D.N.Y.) 4.14
Kepner-Tregoe Inc. v. Leadership Software Inc. 29 USPQ 2d 1747 (C.A. 5, 1994). 4.25
Lewis Galoob Toys Inc. v. Nintendo of America Inc. 20 USPQ 2d 1662, 22 I.P.R. 379 (N.D. Calif. 1991); 22 USPQ 2d 1857 (C.A. 9, 1992) 4.26
MAI Systems Corp. v. Peak Computer Inc. 26 USPQ 2d 1458; [1993] *EIPR* D-141 (C.A. 9, April 7, 1993) 4.25
National Cable Television Assn. v. BMI 772 F. Supp. 614, 20 USPQ 2d 1481 (D.D.C. 1991) 45.90
National Football League v. McBee and Bruno's Inc. 792 F. 2d 726 (C.A. 8, 1986) . 45.90
NBC v. Satellite Broadcast Networks Inc. 940 F. 2d 1467, 19 USPQ 2d 1071 (C.A. 11, 1991) 45.90
On Command Video Corp. v. Columbia Pictures Inc. 777 F. Supp. 787, 21 USPQ 2d 1545 (N.D. Calif. 1991) 45.90
Parfums Givenchy Inc. v. C & C Beauty Sales Inc. 29 USPQ 2d 1026 (C.D. Calif. 1993) 45.90
Prophet Music Inc. v. Shamla Oil Co. Inc. 26 USPQ 2d 1554 (D. Minn. 1993) .. 45.90
Sega Entertainments Ltd. v. Accolade Inc. 977 F. 2d 1510 (C.A. 9, 1993) 4.25
U.S. v. Hux 19 USPQ 2d 1541 (C.A. 8, 1991) 7.42
U.S. Sporting Products Inc. v. Johnny Stewart Game Calls Inc. (Texas C.A. 1993, 1993 Tex. App Lexis 2675, summary in [1994] *Ent. L.R.* E-12) 45.90
Whelan v. Jaslow 230 USPQ 481 (C.A. 3, 1986) 4.25

European Court of Justice

Patricia Im- und Export Verwaltungs-GmbH and anor v. EMI Electrola GmbH [1993] 3 C.M.L.R. 773, [1994] F.S.R. 166; French text *RIDA* 158, 304; German text *GRUR Int.* 1994, 53 .... 7.38
Ministère Public v. Tournier [1991] 4 C.M.L.R. 248 .... 7.38
Phil Collins v. IMTRAT Handels-GmbH [1993] 3 C.M.L.R. 773, [1994] F.S.R. 166; French text *RIDA* 158, 304; German text *GRUR Int.* 1994, 53. . . . 7.38

Correction GVL. v. Commission. In the main text the page reference to *GRUR Int.* 1983 is 734.

TABLE OF INTERNATIONAL TREATIES, CONVENTIONS AND AGREEMENTS

1886 Berne. Convention for the Protection of Literary and Artistic Works (September 9, 1886)
    Paris Revision (1896) 42.00
    Berlin Revision (1908) 28.60
    Paris Revision (1971) . . 7.52, 7.53, 7.55, 20.11
    Art. 2. . . . . 7.50, 7.55
    Art. 7(1). 7.51C, 26.50
        (2) 26.50
        (8) 7.51C
    Art. 9 . . . . 7.55
    Art. 11 . . . . 7.51A
        (1)(ii) 43.70
    Art. 11 *bis* 7.51A
        (1)(ii) 43.70
    Art. 18. . . . . 7.52, 7.55
    Arts II, III of Appendix . . 26.00
1952 Universal Copyright Convention (Geneva). 20.11
    Paris Revision (1971) 20.11
1961 Rome: International Convention for the Protection of Performers, Producers of Phonograms and Broadcasting Organisations (October 26, 1961). 7.46, 7B.07, 20.11, 42.00
    Art. 3(f). 7.51A
    Art. 4(b) 30.20
    Art. 5(1)(c) 30.20
    Art. 7. . . . . 7.51A, 7.52, 28.60, 42.00, 44.30
    Art. 10. . . . 7.51A, 7.52, 28.60
    Art. 12 . . 7.51A, 7A.10, 20.21, 22.30, 23.80, 28.50, 28.60, 29.20, 37.70, 41.10, 43.70, 44.30
    Art. 13 . . . . 7.51A, 7.52

1961 Rome: International Convention for the Protection of Performers, Producers of Phonograms and Broadcasting Organisations—*cont.*
    Art. 14 . . . . 41.80
    Art. 16(1)(a) 22.30
    Art. 19 . . . . 7.50, 41.10
1967 Stockholm Convention establishing the World Intellectual Property Organisation (July 14, 1967) 20.11
1971 Geneva. Convention for the Protection of Producers of Phonograms against Unauthorised Duplication of their Phonograms (October 29, 1971). 7.47, 7.55, 20.11
1974 Brussels. Convention relating to the Distribution of Programme-Carrying Signals Transmitted by Satellite (May 21, 1974) 20.12
1989 Geneva. Treaty on the International Registration of Audiovisual Works (April 20, 1989). 7.49
1992 North American Free Trade Agreement 7.55
    Art. 1701. . . . . 7.55
    Art. 1703. . . . . 7.55
    Art. 1704. . . . . 7.55
    Art. 1705. . . . . 7.55
    Art. 1706. . . . . 7.55
    Art. 1707. . . . . 7.55
    Art. 1708. . . . . 7.55
    Art. 1709. . . . . 7.55
    Art. 1710. . . . . 7.55

1992 North American Free Trade Agreement—*cont.*	
Art. 1712.	7.55
Art. 1713.	7.55
Arts. 1715–1717	7.55
Art. 1718.	7.55
Art. 1719.	7.55
Art. 1720.	7.55
Art. 1721.	7.55
Annexe 1701.3.	7.55
Annexe 1705.3.	7.55
1993 Agreement on Trade-Related Aspects of Intellectual Property Rights, including Trade in Counterfeit Goods (text of December 15, 1993)	7.52
Art. 1	7.52
Art. 2	7.52
Art. 3	7.52
Art. 4	7.52
Art. 9	7.52
Art. 10	7.52
Art. 11	7.52
Art. 12	7.52
Art. 14	7.52
Arts. 15–21	7.52
Arts. 22–26	7.52
Arts. 27–34	7.52
Arts. 35–38	7.52

1993 Agreement on Trade-Related Aspects of Intellectual Property Rights, including Trade in Counterfeit Goods—*cont.*	
Art. 39	7.52
Art. 40	7.52
Arts. 41–61	7.52
Art. 62	7.52
Arts. 63–64	7.52
Arts. 65–67	7.52
Arts. 68–73	7.52
1994 Strasbourg. European Convention relating to Questions on Copyright Law and Neighbouring Rights in the Framework of Transfrontier Broadcasting by Satellite (February 16, 1994)	7.50
Art. 3(1)	7.50
(2)	7.50
(3)	7.50
Art. 4(1)	7.50
(2)	7.50
Art. 5	7.50
(4)	7.50
Art. 6	7.50
9(1)	7.50

TABLE OF EUROPEAN MATERIALS

European Treaties
1957 Rome. Treaty establishing the European Economic Community (March 25, 1957) ... 7.38
    Art. 7(1). 7.38, 7.51C
    Arts. 85–86 . . . . 7.38

Directives (EEC)

1992 Council Directive on rental right and lending right and on certain rights related to copyright in the field of intellectual property (92/100/EEC) [1992] O.J. L346/61 . . . . 7.46, 7.51, 7.51A, 7.51D, 7A.10, 7B.21, 7B.23, 7B.24, 7C.06, 20.20, 20.22, 20.25, 20.31, 23.30, 27.80, 29.30, 30.20, 30.50, 32.60, 32.90, 35.00, 37.70, 40.40, 43.00, 45.70
    Art. 1(1) 7.51A
        (2) 7.51A
        (3) 7.51A
        (4) 7.51A
    Art. 2(1) 7.51A
        (2) 7.51A
        (4) 7.51A
        (5) 7.51A
        (7) 7.51A
    Art. 4 . . . . 7.51A
        (1)(2) 7.51A
    Art. 6 . . . . 7.51A
        (1) 7.51A
    Art. 7(1) 7.51A
    Art. 8(1) 7.51A
        (2) 7.51A
    Art. 9(1)(2) 7.51A

Directives (EEC)—*cont.*
    Art. 13 . . . . 7.51A
        (1) 7.51A
    Art. 15 . . . . 7.51A
1993 Council Directive on the co-ordination of certain rules concerning copyright and rights related to copyright applicable to satellite broadcasting and cable retransmission (93/83/EEC) [1993] O.J. L248/15 . . . . . . 7.51, 7.51B, 7.51D, 23.20, 27.80, 29.30, 30.20, 30.50, 32.60, 32.90, 35.00, 37.70, 40.40, 43.00, 45.70
    Art. 1(2) 7.51B
        (2)(a) 7.51B
        (2)(b) 7.51B
        (2)(d) 7.51B
    Art. 2 . . . . 7.51B
    Art. 3 . . . . 7.51B
        (1) 7.51B
    Art. 4 . . . . 7.51B
    Art. 8 . . . . 7.51B
    Art. 9 . . . . 7.51B
    Art. 10 . . . . 7.51B
    Art. 11 . . . . 7.51B
    Art. 12 . . . . 7.51B
    Art. 14(1) 7.51B
1993 Council Directive harmonising the term of protection of copyright and certain related rights (93/98/EEC) [1993] O.J. L290/9 . . . 7.51, 7.51C, 7.51D, 7B.22, 20.20, 23.30, 27.80, 29.30, 30.20, 30.50, 32.60, 32.90, 35.00, 37.70, 40.40, 43.00, 45.70

Directives (EEC)—*cont.*

Art. 1 . . . . .7.51C
Art. 2(1) 7.51C
    (2) 7.51C
Art. 3 . . . . .7.51C
    (1) 7.51C
    (2) 7.51C
    (3) 7.51C
    (4) 7.51C
Art. 7 . . . . .7.51C
    (2) 7.51C
Art. 9 . . . . .7.51C
Art. 10(2) 7.51C
    (3) 7.51C
    (4) 7.51C
    (5) 7.51C

Draft Directive (EEC)

1993 Amended proposal for a Council Directive on the legal protection of databases [1993] O.J. C308/1 . . . . .7.51D

Regulation (EEC)

1986 Council Regulation on measures to prohibit the release for free circulation of counterfeit goods No. 3842/86 of December 1 [1986] O.J. L357/1 . . . . 7.42

Draft Regulation (EEC)

1993 E.C. Commission proposal for Council Regulation on measures to prohibit the release for free circulation, export or transit of counterfeit and pirated goods (COM(93)329 final) [1993] O.J. C238/9 . . 7.42

Recommendation (Council of Europe)

1991 Recommendation No. R(91)14 of September 27 on the legal protection of encrypted television services 7.50

Convention (Council of Europe): *see* **Table of International Treaties, Conventions and Agreements (1994)**

Agreement

1992 European Economic Area Agreement 7.54
    Art. 65(2) 7.54
    Protocol 28 . . . . 7.54
    Annex XVII. 7.54

TABLE OF LEGISLATIVE INSTRUMENTS

Albania

1993 Law on Author's Right, No.
      7564 of May 19 . . . . . 21.20

Angola

1990 Law on Author's Right, No.
      4/90 of March 10 . . . . 21.60
      art. 32 . . . . 21.60
      art. 36 . . . . 21.60

Australia

1968 Copyright Act 22.30
      s. 85 . . . . 22.30
      s. 89 . . . . 22.30
      ss. 108–109 . . . . 22.30
1989 Copyright Amendment Act . 22.30
1991 Copyright Amendment Act . 22.30

Austria

1936 Law of April 9
      art. 16(3) 20.31
      art. 16a 20.31
          (1)–(3) 20.31
          (5) 20.31
      art. 67(2) 20.31
      art. 74(7) 20.31
      art. 76(6) 20.31
      art. 76a(5) 20.31
1988 Amendment Law No. 601 . . 22.60
1989 Amendment Law No. 612 . . 22.60
1993 Amending Law UrhRGNov
      1993 (93) 20.31, 22.60

Bahrain

1993 Decree No. 10/1993 . . . . . . 22.95
      art. 6 . . . . 22.95
      art. 22 . . . . 22.95
      art. 35 . . . . 22.95

Belgium

1953 Law of July 27 . . . . 23.30

Bolivia

Penal Code
      art. 362 . . . . 23.80
1992 Law No. 1322 of April
      13 . . . . 20.31, 23.80
      art. 5(ñ) 23.80
      art. 19 . . . . 23.80
      art. 30 . . . . 23.80
      art. 40 . . . . 23.80
      art. 41 . . . . 23.80
      art. 43 . . . . 23.80
      art. 53 . . . . 23.80
      art. 54 . . . . 23.80
      art. 55 . . . . 23.80
      art. 56 . . . . 23.80
      arts. 65–70 . . . . 23.80

Bulgaria

1951 Law of November 16
      art. 16 . . . . 24.70
1990 Law of March 30 . . . . 20.31
1991 Decree No. 19 of February
      13 . . . . 24.70

1993 Law on Author's Right and
 Neighbouring Rights
 of June 16 . . . . 24.70
 art. 18(2)(2). 20.31
 art. 21. . . . . 24.70
 art. 22. . . . . 24.70
 art. 26. . . . . 20.28
  (2). 20.28
 art. 62(1). 24.70
  (2). 24.70
 art. 63(1)(2). 24.70
 art. 75. . . . . 24.70
 art. 76(1) 20.31, 24.70
  (2) 24.70
  (3) 24.70
 art. 77. . . . . 24.70
 art. 78. . . . . 24.70
 art. 82. . . . . 24.70
 art. 86. . . . . 24.70
  (1)(1). 20.31
 art. 88. . . . . 24.70
 art. 94. . . . . 24.70
 art. 95. . . . . 24.70
 art. 97. . . . . 24.70
 art. 98(4). 24.70
 Additional provisions
 art. 2(4). 20.31
 art. 3. . . . . 20.31

1992 Miscellaneous Statute Law
 Amendment Act,
 c. 1. . . . . 25.30
1993 Intellectual Property Law
 Improvement Act,
 c. 15. . . . . 25.30
1993 An Act to amend the Copyright Act, c. 23 . . . . . 25.30
1993 North American Free Trade
 Agreement Implemen-
 tation Act, c. 44. . . . . 20.31,
  25.30

Chile

1970 Law No. 17.336/1970
 art. 67. . . . . 25.90
 art. 68 . . . . 20.31, 25.90
1992 Law No. 19.166 of September 9 . . . . 25.90
 art. 1(1)(3). 25.90
  (9) 20.31, 25.90
 art. 8. . . . . 25.90
 art. 9. . . . . 25.90
 art. 10. . . . . 25.90

Canada

1921 Copyright Act as amended to
 December 31, 1989. . . . . . .
  20.31, 25.30
 s. 2. . . . . 25.30
  (1)(h) 20.31
 s. 3(1) 25.30
  (f). 25.30
  (1.4). 25.30
  (4) 25.30
 s. 5(1) 25.30
  (4). 20.31, 25.30
 s. 6 . . . . 25.30
 s. 10(1) 25.30
 s. 11.1 . . . . 25.30
 s. 13(3) 25.30
 s. 22 . . . . 25.30
1990 Integrated Circuit Topography Act, c. 37 . . . . 25.30

China

1986 General Principles of Civil
 Law 26.00
1990 Law of September 7 . . . . . 26.00
 art. 2. . . . . 26.00
 art. 9(5). 20.31
 art. 20. . . . . 26.00
 art. 21. . . . . 26.00
 art. 39. . . . . 26.00
 art. 43. . . . . 26.00
1991 Implementing Regulations of
 May 24. . . . . 26.00
 art. 5 . . . . 20.31, 26.00
 art. 47. . . . . 26.00
1991 Computer Software Regulations 26.00
1992 Rules for the Registration of
 Protectible Software . . 26.00

1992 International Copyright
        Treaties Implementing
        Rules of September
        25 . . . . 26.00
    art. 3. . . . . 26.00
    art. 4. . . . . 26.00
    art. 5. . . . . 26.00
    arts. 5–7 . . . . 26.00
    art. 12. . . . . 26.00
    art. 14. . . . . 26.00
    art. 15. . . . . 26.00
    art. 17. . . . . 26.00
    art. 18. . . . . 26.00

Colombia

1982 Law No. 23 of January 28
    art. 27. . . . . 26.50
    art. 29. . . . . 26.50
    art. 96. . . . . 26.50
1993 Amending Law No. 44 of
        February 4 . . . . 26.50
    arts. 51–54 . . . . 26.50
    art. 69. . . . . 26.50

Cyprus

1976 Law No. 59 of December 3 . 27.50
    s. 7(1) 27.50
    s. 13(4) 27.50
    s. 14A 27.50
1993 Copyright (Amendment)
        Act 20.31, 27.50

Czechoslovakia

1965 Law No. 35 of March 25
    art. 45(2)(3). 27.60

Czech Republic

1965 Law No. 35 of March 25 . . 27.70

1965 Law No. 35 of March 25—*cont.*
    art. 13(2). 20.31
    art. 16. . . . . 27.70
    art. 44. . . . . 20.31
1990 Law No. 89 of March
        28 . . . . 20.31, 27.70
1991 Decree 115/1991 of March
        15 . . . . 27.70, 42.65
1991 Federal Law No. 468 of
        November 1 . . 20.31, 27.70

Denmark

1961 Law No. 158 of May 31, as
        amended to June 7,
        1989 (Consolidation
        Law) 20.31, 27.80
    art. 22a 27.80
    art. 42. . . . . 43.60
1992 Amending Law No. 338 of
        May 14 . . . . . 20.28, 27.80

Ecuador

1992 Law No. 161 of July 14. . . . 28.30

Egypt

1954 Law No. 354 of June 24 . . . 28.40
    art. 2. . . . . 28.40
    art. 20. . . . . 28.40
1977 Presidential Decree 442/
        1977. . . . . 28.40
1992 Amending Law No. 38 of
        June 4 . . . . 28.40
    art. 47. . . . . 28.40
1993 Ministerial Decree No. 162/
        1993. . . . . 28.40

El Salvador

1993 Decree 604 of July 15 . . . . . 28.50
    art. 7(d). 20.31

1993 Decree 604 of July 15—*cont.*
    art. 8, 9(d) 28.50
    art. 81 . . . . 28.50
    art. 83 . . . . 20.31

Estonia

1992 Law on author's right of November 11 . . . . 28.60
    art. 13(2) 20.31
    art. 27 . . . . 20.28, 28.60
    art. 33 . . . . 28.60
    art. 66 . . . . 28.60
    art. 67(1) 28.60
    art. 70(2) 20.31
    art. 72 . . . . 28.60
    arts. 79–81 . . . . 28.60

Finland

1961 Law No. 404 of July 8 . . . . . 29.20
    art. 39 . . . . 43.60
    art. 45 . . . . 29.20
    art. 46 . . . . 29.20
    art. 47 . . . . 29.20
1991 Law No. 34 of January 11 . . . . 20.31, 29.20

France

1957 Law No. 57-298 of March 11
    art. 1(1) 20.31
    art. 31(3) 20.31
1985 Law No. 85-660 of July 3
    art. 21 . . . . 20.31
    art. 26 . . . . 20.31
    arts. 31–37 . . . . 20.28
1992 Law No. 92-546 of June 20 . 29.30
1992 Code of Intellectual Property (CIP): Law No. 92-597 of July 1 . . . . 29.30
    L.111.1 . . . . 20.31
    L.131.3 . . . . 20.31
    L.213.1 . . . . 20.31

1992 Code of Intellectual Property (CIP): Law No. 92-597 of July 1—*cont.*
    L.215.1 . . . . 20.31
    L.311 . . . . 20.28
    L.311.6 . . . . 20.28
    L.311.7 . . . . 20.28

(The following list shows the CIP articles corresponding to those of the 1957 Law quoted in the main text.)

1957 Law	CIP
art. 1	L.111.1
art. 2	L.112.1
art. 3 (*refer also to para 5.37*)	L.112.2
art. 4	L.112.3
art. 14	L.113.7
art. 17	L.132.23
art. 18	L.113.8
art. 19	L.121.2
art. 21	L.123.1 and L.123.2
art. 22	L.123.3
art. 26	L.122.1
art. 27	L.122.2
art. 27(2)	L.122.2
art. 28	L.122.3
art. 31(3)	L.131.3, 4
art. 45	L.132.20
art. 63(1)	L.132.24
art. 81	L.811.1

1985 Law	CIP
art. 9	(L.122.2)
art. 12	(L.132.20)
art. 15	L.211.1, 211.2
art. 16	L.212.1
art. 18	L.212.3
art. 19	L.212.4–.7
art. 21	L.213.1
art. 22	L.214.1
art. 26	L.215.1
art. 27	L.216.1
art. 28	L.311.2
art. 29	L.211.3, 212.10
art. 31–37	L.311
art. 63	L.811.1

(*Corrections to main text Table*. The references to article 108 of the 1957 Law and article 80 of the 1985 Law should be

Table of Legislative Instruments

deleted. The reference to article 3 under the 1985 Law should be to article 3 of the 1957 Law (para. 5.37). The reference relating to article 9 under the 1985 Law should be to paragraph 7.26. There should be an additional reference to paragraph 5.37 under the 1985 Law, article 21.)

Germany

1965	Law of September 9	
	art. 120(1)	7.51C
	art. 125(1)	7.38, 7.51C
	art. 125((2)–(6)	7.38
	art. 126(1)	7.51C
	art. 127(1)	7.51C
1993	Law of June 9	30.20

Greece

1986	Law No. 1597	
	art. 3(1)	30.50
1993	Law No. 2121 of March 3	30.50
	art. 1	30.50
	art. 2(1)	30.50
	(2)	30.50
	art. 3(1)(d)	20.31
	(1)(g)	30.50
	art. 8	30.50
	art. 9	30.50
	art. 18	30.50
	(1)	20.28
	(3)	20.28
	art. 34	30.50
	art. 34(4)	20.31
	art. 35(2)	30.50
	(3)	30.50
	art. 43	30.50
	art. 46(2)(b)	20.31
	(2)(c)(d)	30.50
	art. 46(3)	30.50
	art. 47(1)	20.31
	art. 48(1)(d)	20.31
	art. 49(1)	30.50
	(4)	30.50
	arts. 59–63	30.50
	art. 64	30.50

1993	Law No. 2121 of March 3—*cont.*	
	art. 65	30.50
	art. 66	30.50
	art. 67(4)	30.50

Honduras

1991	Law No. 131-91 of October 22	31.70
	art. 1	31.70
	art. 4	31.70
	art. 5	31.70
	art. 6	31.70

Hungary

1993	Amendment to Penal Code of March 2	31.90
1994	Law on neighbouring rights, of February 8	31.90

Iceland

1992	Amending Law of May 19	32.10

India

1991	Copyright (Amendment) Ordinance No. 9	32.20

Isle of Man

1991	Copyright Act 1991, c. 8	32.70
	s. 18(1)	20.31
	(2)	20.31
	ss. 96–102	32.70
	s. 106	32.70

Italy

1941 Law No. 663 of April
22 . . . . 20.31, 32.90
    art. 73. . . . . .32.90
1992 Law No. 93 of February
5 . . . . 20.28, 32.90

Jamaica

1993 Copyright Act 33.10
    s. 2(1) 20.31, 33.10
    s. 3(2). 20.31
    s. 6(1) 33.10
    s. 9(d) 33.10
    s. 14 . . . . .33.10
    s. 15 . . . . .33.10
    ss. 29–43. . . . . .33.10
    s. 46 . . . . .33.10
    s. 108 . . . . .33.10
    s. 109 . . . . .33.10
    ss. 112–114 . . . . .33.10
    ss. 135A–135G 33.10

Japan

1970 Law No. 48 of May 6
    art. 101. . . . . .33.20
1991 Law (Amendments) No. 63
of May 2. . . . . 20.32, 33.20
    art. 4. . . . . .33.20
    art. 121*bis*. 33.20
1992 Amending Law No. 106 of
December 16 . . . . .33.20
    art. 30(2). 20.28
    art. 102. . . . . .20.28
    arts. 104*bis*–104*quater*. .20.28
    art. 104*sexies*. 20.28
    art. 104*octies*. 20.28

Jordan

1912 Law of May 8 (Ottoman) . . 7.05,
33.30

1992 Law No. 22 of April 16. . . . 7.05,
33.30
    art. 5. . . . . .33.30
    art. 8. . . . . .33.30
    art. 23. . . . . .33.30
    art. 37. . . . . .33.30
    art. 45. . . . . .33.30
    arts. 46–50 . . . . .33.30
    art. 53. . . . . .33.30

Latvia

1993 Law on Author's Right and
Neighbouring Rights, of
May 11 . . . . .34.35
    art. 11(1). 34.35
    (2) 34.35
    art. 12. . . . . .34.35
    art. 14(2)(2). 20.31
    (7) 34.35
    art. 40(1)(7). 20.31
    (4) 20.31
    art. 43(1). 20.31
    (4) 20.31
    art. 51. . . . . .20.31
    arts. 54–57 . . . . .34.35

Malta

1967 Copyright Act 36.00
    s. 2(1) 36.00
1992 Act No. 20. . . . . .36.00

Mexico

1991 Decree of July 9 . . . . .36.50

Netherlands

1912 Author's Right Law of September 23 . . . . .37.70
    art. 16(c)–(g) . . . 20.28, 37.70

1989 Civil Code
    art. 6(12)............37.70
1990 Law. No 305, of May 30...20.28
1993 Law on Neighbouring
    Rights, of March 18......37.70
    art. 1...............37.70
    art. 7...............37.70
    art. 10..............20.28
    art. 16..............37.70
    art. 17..............37.70
    arts. 21–31 ....37.70

Niger

1993 Law No. 93/93..........38.40

Nigeria

1988 Copyright Decree
    s. 32C..............20.28
    s. 39...............38.50
1992 Copyright (Amendment) Decree (Decree No. 98 of December 28)..... 20.28, 38.50

Norway

1961 Law of May 12
    art. 39..............43.60
    art. 54..............38.90

Poland

1994 Author's Right and Neighbouring Rights Law, February 4..................40.30

Portugal

1985 Code on Author's Right and Related Rights, No. 45/85 of September 17...........40.40

1991 Amending Law No. 114/91 of September 3..........40.40

Russian Federation

1992 Resolution of the Supreme Soviet of July 14 (Civil Legal Relations).............41.10
1992 Law of September 23 (Semiconductor Topographies)...41.10
1992 Law of September 23 (Computer Programs and Databases).................41.10
1993 Law of July 9, 1993, on Author's Right and Neighbouring Rights..........41.10
    art. 3...............41.10
    art. 4...............41.10
    art. 7(2)(3)..........41.10
    art. 9...............41.10
    art. 13(1)...........41.10
        (2)............41.10
    art. 14..............41.10
    art. 15..............41.10
        (3)............41.10
    art. 16..............41.10
        (2)............20.31
    art. 17..............41.10
    art. 25..............41.10
    art. 26..............20.28
        (2)............20.28
        (3)............20.28
    art. 27(1)...........41.10
    art. 28.............. 7.09
    art. 37(1)–(3)........41.10
        (2)(5).........20.31
        (6)............41.10
    art. 38..............41.10
        (1)............41.10
        (2)............41.10
        (2)(3).........20.31
    art. 39..............41.10
        (1)............41.10
        (2)............41.10
        (2)–(4)........41.10
    art. 40..............41.10
    art. 41..............41.10
    art. 43(1)...........41.10
        (2)............41.10
        (3)(4).........41.10
    art. 48..............41.10

1993 Law of July 9, 1993, on Author's Right and Neighbouring Rights—*cont.*
    art. 49(1)(5).......... 41.10
    art. 49(2)............. 41.10
    art. 49(4)............. 41.10
    art. 50................ 41.10
1993 Resolution of the Supreme Soviet of the Russian Federation of July 9 .... 41.10

St. Vincent and the Grenadines

1989 Copyright Act (Act No. 53) of December 27 .... 41.80
    s. 2 .... 20.31, 41.80
    s. 3 .... 41.80
    s. 5(1) 41.80
    s. 12(3) 41.80
    s. 13(c) 41.80
    s. 14 .... 41.80
    s. 25(1) 41.80
    s. 30 .... 41.80
        (1)(a), (5) 41.80
    s. 33 .... 41.80
    s. 45 .... 20.31

San Marino

1991 Law No. 8 of January 25... 42.00
    art. 1................. 42.00
    art. 5................. 42.00
        (b)............. 42.00
    art. 6(c).............. 42.00
    art. 10................ 42.00
    art. 20................ 42.00
    art. 23................ 42.00
    art. 24................ 42.00
    art. 25................ 42.00
    arts. 27–31 .... 42.00
    art. 32................ 42.00
    art. 42................ 42.00
    art. 44................ 42.00
    art. 45................ 42.00
    art. 62................ 42.00
    arts. 67–70 .... 42.00
    art. 93................ 42.00

1991 Law No. 8 of January 15—*cont.*
    art. 94............. 42.00
    art. 95............. 42.00
    art. 97............. 42.00
    arts. 112–120........ 42.00

Saudi Arabia

1992 Royal Decree M/26 of March 11................... 42.20

Seychelles

1982 Copyright Act 42.40
1984 Copyright (Registration) Regulations 42.40

Slovak Republic

1965 Law No. 35 of March 25 .... 42.65
    art. 16.............. 42.65
1990 Law No. 89 of March 28 ..42.65
1991 Federal Law No. 468 of November 1............ 42.65

South Africa

1965 Copyright Act 37.40
1967 Performers Protection Act ..37.40
1992 Copyright Amendment Act .42.90

Spain

1987 Law 22/1987 of November 11.................... 43.00
    art. 25 .... 20.28, 43.00
        (4)............ 20.28

TABLE OF LEGISLATIVE INSTRUMENTS

1987 Law 22/1987 of November 11—cont.
    art. 25(5)–(10) 20.28
    art. 103 . . . . 43.00
    art. 127 . . . . 43.00
1991 Royal Decree 1584/1991 . . . 43.00
1992 Law 20/1992 of July 7 . . . . 20.28, 43.00
1992 Decree No. 1434/92 of November 27 . . . . . 20.28, 43.00

Sweden

1960 Law No. 729 of December 30 . . . . 43.60
    art. 39 . . . . 43.60
1986 Law No. 367 of June 5 . . . . 29.20
1991 Law of June 20 . . . . 43.60
1992 Law No. 1685 . . . . 43.60

Switzerland

1922 Law of December 7 . . . . 43.70
1992 Law of October 9 . . . . 43.70
    art. 2(3) 43.70
    art 10(2)(d) 43.70
        (2)(e) 43.70
        (3) 20.31
    art. 13(1) 20.31, 43.70
        (3) 20.31
    art. 19 . . . . 20.28
    art. 20(3) 20.28, 43.70
        (4) 20.28
    art. 22(1) 43.70
        (2) 43.70
        (3) 43.70
    art. 29(2)(a) 43.70
    art. 30(3) 43.70
    art. 33 . . . . 43.70
        (2)(b) 43.70
    art. 35(1) 7A.05, 43.70
        (2) 43.70
        (3) 43.70
        (4) 43.70
    art. 36 . . . . 43.70
    arts. 40–66 . . . . 43.70
    arts. 61–66 . . . . 43.70

Taiwan

1928 Law of May 14 . . . . 44.00
1928 Implementation Rules of the Copyright Law, of May 14, 1928, as amended to June 10 1992 . . . . 44.00
    art. 74 . . . . 44.00
    art. 75 . . . . 44.00
1992 Law of June 10 . . . . 44.00
    art. 3(1) 44.00
        (7) 44.00
        5(7) 20.31
        (8) 20.31, 44.00
        (10) 44.00
    art. 11 . . . . 44.00
    art. 12 . . . . 44.00
    art. 29 . . . . 20.31
    art. 33 . . . . 44.00
    art. 34 . . . . 44.00
    arts. 84–90 . . . . 44.00
    arts. 91–104 . . . . 44.00
1992 Rules of June 10 (content of works) 44.00
1992 Rules of June 10 (royalty rates) 44.00
1992 Regulations of June 10 (compulsory licence of translation rights) 44.00
1992 Regulations of June 10 (compulsory licence of musical works) 44.00
1992 Amending Law of July 6 . . . 44.00
1992 Organic Charter of August 28 (Copyright Examination and Mediation Committee) . 44.00
1992 Regulations of September 23 (copyright dispute mediation) 44.00
1993 Amending Law of April 24 . 44.00
1993 Rules of April 24 (article 87*bis*) of the Copyright Law 44.00

Thailand

1978 Law of December 8
    s. 8 . . . . 44.20

Togo

1991 Law No. 91-12 of June 10...44.30
    art. 6(xiv)............44.30
    art. 9................44.30
    art. 10...............44.30
    art. 96...............44.30
    art. 103..............44.30
    art. 106..............44.30
    Arts. 112–114.........44.30
    art. 116..............44.30

Tunisia

1966 Law No. 66-12 of February 14....................44.80

Union of Soviet Socialist Republics

1991 Fundamentals of Civil Legislation (Title IV) of May 31 . 41.10

United Arab Emirates

1992 Federal Law No. 40 of September 28..............45.60
    art. 26...............45.60
    art. 29...............45.60

United Kingdom

1911 Copyright Act (1 & 2 Geo. 5 (1911) c. 46)
    s. 1(1)...............25.30
1956 Copyright Act (4 & 5 Eliz. 2 (1955–56) c. 74)...25.30, 32.70, 37.40, 41.80

1988 Copyright, Designs and Patents Act (c. 48)...32.70, 33.10, 45.70
    s. 159................32.70
1991 Criminal Justice Act
    s. 18.................45.70

Statutory Instruments

1992 Copyright (Isle of Man) (Revocation) Order 1992 (S.I. 1992 No. 1306)......32.70
    Copyright (Application to the Isle of Man) Order 1992 (S.I. 1992 No. 1313)......32.70
    45.70
1992 Copyright (Computer Programs) Regulations 1992 (S.I. 1992 No. 3233)......45.70

United States of America

1976 Copyright Act (PL94-553)..41.80, 42.00, 45.90
    s. 101................45.90
    s. 106................45.90
    s. 109(a).............45.90
    s. 110(5).............45.90
    (5)(B)................45.90
    s. 111................45.90
    ss. 1001–1010.........20.28
    s. 1002...............45.90
    s. 1004...............20.28
    s. 1006(b)(1).........20.28
    (b)(2)................20.28
    s. 1008...............20.28
    s. 1009...............45.90
1990 Architectural Works Copyright Protection Act (PL101-650)..................45.90
1992 Amending Act of October 28 (PL102-561)............45.90
1992 Audio Home Recording Act (PL102-563)......20.28, 45.90
1993 North American Free Trade Agreement Implementation Act (PL103-182).........45.90

Table of Legislative Instruments

Venezuela

1993 Law of August 14 . . . . 46.60	
art. 5 . . . . 46.60	
art. 12 . . . . 46.60	
art. 14 . . . . 46.60	
art. 15 . . . . 20.31, 46.60	
art. 26 . . . . 46.60	
art. 39 . . . . 46.60	

1993 Law of August 14—*cont.*
    art. 41 . . . . 20.31
    art. 43 . . . . 46.60
    art. 59 . . . . 46.60
    art. 92 . . . . 46.60
    art. 95 . . . . 20.31
    art. 97 . . . . 46.60
    art. 98 . . . . 46.60
    arts. 109–118 . . . . 46.60
    arts. 119–124 . . . . 46.60

PART I

COMMENTARY

CHAPTER 3

RECORDING DESCRIPTIONS

"Production" and "work"

At the end of the third paragraph in the main text, insert "See further paragraph 5.17."   **3.02**

Computer-simulated actors

For a survey of the questions concerning computer produced re-animations of actors see Beard, J.L., "Casting call at Forest Lawn: the digital resurrection of deceased entertainers—a 21st Century challenge for intellectual property law" 41 *J. Copr. Soc'y 19* (1993) and, by the same author, "Computer generated synthetic actors—a novel challenge for copyright law" *Copyright World* 1994, March, 24.   **3.24**

CHAPTER 4

RECORDING USES AND CORRESPONDING RIGHTS

Sampling, re-mastering and colourisation

Sampling

On a French case concerning sampling, and general consideration of the problem, see Logie, Ph., "The Dechavanne case: unauthorised sound sampling of a distinctive voice" [1993] *Ent. L.R.*, 121.   **4.14**

For a United States case concerning sampling of quotations of songs, see *Grand Upright Music Ltd. v. Warner Brothers Records Inc. et al* [1992] *Ent. L.R.* E–27 (S.D.N.Y.).

For a detailed survey see Bently, L. and Sherman, B., "Cultures of copying: digital sampling and copyright law" [1992] *Ent. L.R.* 158. See also Du Bois, R. "The legal aspects of sound sampling" *UNESCO Cop. Bull.* 1992, XXVI/2/7, and Gringras, C. "Copyright in sound recordings in the United Kingdom" *Copyright World* 1994, March, 31.

B. National law examples

4.17 **The Australian Apple case** Footnote 21(c) in the main text: as to developments concerning the decision in *Whelan v. Jaslow*, see paragraph 4.25.

4.24 The decision of the Court of Appeals, Eleventh Circuit, in *Bellsouth Advertising and Publishing Corp. v. Donnelly Information Publishing Inc.* 19 USPQ 2d 1345 was vacated: on the rehearing, the Court reversed the earlier decision, holding that the defendant had not infringed the plaintiff's copyright in storing the information and reprinting the plaintiff's directories (28 USPQ 2d 1001 (U.S.C.A. 11, 1993)). However, the finding that storage in the computer constituted copying was not specifically mentioned or overruled by the Appeals Court. The case represents an interesting survey of the developments regarding the decision in *Feist* (see main text para. 6.20).

Program infringement

Australia

4.25 The extent of copyright protection in respect of a computer "lock" was considered in *Autodesk Inc. and Another v. Dyason and Others* [1993] R.P.C. 259 (High Court). See comment by Bodger, A. in [1992] *EIPR* 211; see also [1993] *EIPR* D–123.

Canada

The abstraction-filtration-comparison test for establishing similarity as adopted in *Computer Associates v. Altai* (see under United States of America, below) was considered in *Delrina Corp. v. Triolet Systems Inc.* (1993) 47 C.P.R. (3d) 1 (Ontario Ct., Gen. Div.), where the various approaches to this question in the context of computer program infringement were considered in detail.

United States of America

In *Computer Associates International Inc. v. Altai Inc.* 775 F. Supp. 544 (E.D.N.Y. 1991); 982 F. 2d 693, 23 USPQ 2d 1241 (U.S.C.A. 2, 1992) (comments by Zadra-Symes, L. in [1992] *EIPR* 327, and see Rinck, G.M., "The maturing U.S. law on copyright protection for computer programs" [1992] *EIPR* 351), the approach of the United States Court of Appeals, Third Circuit, in *Whelan v. Jaslow* 230 USPQ 481 was rejected by the Second Circuit, which adopted a test of abstraction-filtration-comparison in assessing similarity in the context of alleged infringement of copyright in a computer program. Nevertheless the possibility of protection of structure-sequence-organisation, though not in the circumstances of *Whelan v. Jaslow*, appears to be confirmed in *Kepner-Tregoe Inc. v. Leadership Software Inc.* 29 USPQ 2d 1747 (U.S.C.A. 5, 1994: see footnote 20).

See generally Karjala, D.S., "Recent United States and international developments in software protection" [1994] *EIPR* 13, 58.

Other cases where the "abstraction-filtration-comparison" test was considered include: *Autoskill Inc. v. National Education Support Systems Inc.* 26 USPQ 2d 1828 (U.S.C.A. 10, 1993); *Gates Rubber Co. v. Bands Chemical Industries Ltd.* 28 USPQ 2d 1503 (U.S.C.A. 10, 1993).

In *Sega Entertainments Ltd. v. Accolade Inc.* 977 F. 2d. 1510 (U.S.C.A. 9, 1993) it was held that decompilation of a computer program constituted copying, but the defendant succeeded on fair use grounds: see comments by Stern, R.H. in [1992] *EIPR* 407, and [1993] *EIPR* 34; see also [1993] *EIPR* D–41 and D–91.

On the extrinsic and intrinsic tests applied to assess whether substantial similarity exists between two programs, and consideration of protectible as well as unprotectible features, see *Brown Bag Software v. Symantec Corp.* 960 F. 2d 1465 (U.S.C.A. 9, 1992; cert. denied October 5, 1992).

Loading a program constitutes copying: *MAI Systems Corp. v. Peak Computer Inc.* 26 USPQ 2d 1458; [1993] *EIPR* D–141 (U.S.C.A. 9, 1993).

Videogames and screen displays 4.26

Germany

For cases concerning protection of a video game under German law, either as a computer program or a cinematographic work, see the cases noted in

[1992] *EIPR* D–176 (OLG Cologne, October 18, 1991) [1992] *EIPR* D–238 (Bay OBLG, May 12, 1992), and [1993] *EIPR* D–105.

South Africa

In *Nintendo Co. Ltd v. Golden China TV Game Centre* (South Africa, Supreme Court, summary in [1994] *Ent. L.R.* E–8, comment by Job, C. in *Copyright World* December 1993/January 1994, 5) it was held that the visual displays of video games generated by computer programs constitute "cinematograph films" within the definition in section 1(1)(viii) of the South African Copyright Act 1978.

United Kingdom

Questions of copyright in screen displays as an artistic work or film, or as a reproduction of a drawing were considered, together with the tests for establishing similarity, in *John Richardson Computers Ltd v. Flanders and Another* [1993] F.S.R. 497 (Ch.D.).

For a detailed survey of the current English law on the protection of computer programs, dealing, *inter alia*, with the protection of program compilations, the protection of detailed ideas and the differences between English and United States law on the protection of functional works, and a detailed analysis of the process of establishing literal and non-literal copying, see the judgment of Jacob J. in *IBCOS Computers Ltd. v. Poole and Others* (Ch. D., February 24, 1994, [1994] F.S.R. 275 (under appeal)).

United States of America

For an analysis of the protectible and unprotectible elements in a screen display, and application of the "extrinsic" and "intrinsic" tests of similarity, see *Apple Computer Inc. v. Microsoft Corp.* 20 USPQ 2d 1236 (N.D. Calif. 1991); 24 USPQ 2d 1081 (N.D.Calif. 1992); 27 USPQ 2d 1081 (N.D.Calif. 1993).

The unique and creative arrangement of instructions in a video game "lock" program held protectible: *Atari Games Corp. v. Nintendo of America Inc.* 24 USPQ 2d 1015 (C.A.F.C. 1992).

In *Lewis Galoob Toys Inc. v. Nintendo of America Inc.* 20 USPQ 2d 1662; 22 I.P.R. 379 (N.D.Calif. 1991); 22 USPQ 2d 1857 (U.S.C.A. 9, 1992), it was held that the result of using a video game accessory which allows the player to alter the video game temporarily did not constitute infringement of the video game copyright by the unauthorised making of a derivative work. For analysis and discussion of the first instance decision see Glick, M. and Page, M., "Copyright protection of video games in the United States" [1992] *EIPR* 24; Stern, R.H., "The Game Genie case: copyright in derivative works versus users' rights" [1992] *Ent. L.R.* 104.

Works which are products of computer programs, such as certain types of screen displays, are considered audiovisual works for copyright purposes, whereas the programs themselves are considered literary works. If a computer generated audiovisual display is copyrighted separately as an audiovisual work apart from the program that generates it, the display may be protectible irrespective of the copyright status of the underlying program: *Computer Associates International Inc. v. Altai Inc.* (see para. 4.25).

As to developments concerning *Whelan v. Jaslow*, see paragraph 4.25.

Meaning of "distribution" 4.45

Parallel Imports

In many countries, the domestic law grants the local rightowner the right to prevent importation of material legitimately produced in a foreign country. In certain jurisdictions, including the United States, relief is obtainable in respect of importation of legitimately produced or pirated material, on the basis of the copyright or author's right in the artistic or literary work in the label or packaging: see paragraphs 22.30, 38.90, 45.90.

The corresponding right

Moral rights

See generally Karnell, G., "The broadcasting of audiovisual works and moral rights" *Copyright World* December 1993/January 1994, 24. 4.69

U.K. 1988 Act

For a case in which a composer obtained an injunction in respect of alleged infringement of his moral right under section 80 of the 1988 Act (claiming derogatory treatment by modification of lyrics, juxtaposition of extracts, etc.) see *Morrison Leahy Music Ltd. & Another v. Lightbond Ltd. &* 4.70

Others [1993] E.M.L.R. 144 ("George Michael: moral right") (Ch.D.); discussed at [1992] *Ent.L.R.* 26.

APPENDIX

COMPUTER LAW AFFECTING RECORDINGS

A. NATIONAL LAWS

I. Subsistence of rights

(c) Author's right system

4A.13 As regards Italy, see also *Industrial Property* 1992, January.

4A.18 (iii) **United States 1976 Act.** For other United States cases concerning videogames, see paragraph 4.25.

(c) U.S. 1976 Act

4A.26 As to developments concerning *Whelan v. Jaslow*, and for United States cases concerning infringement of program copyright, see paragraph 4.25. As to *Bellsouth Advertising v. Donnelly*, see paragraph 4.24. For other United States cases concerning screen displays, see paragraph 4.26.

CHAPTER 6

BASIS AND STRUCTURE OF PROTECTION

Nature of produced recordings

6.01 On the history of protection of the sound recording and the moves for its inclusion in the Berne Convention, see Boytha, G., "The intellectual property status of sound recordings" *IIC* 1993, 295, and on the development of protection of sound recordings, see Cornish, W., "Sound recordings and copyright" *IIC* 1993, 306.

United States of America

(i) *General basis*

As to developments concerning *Whelan v. Jaslow*, see paragraph 4.25. 6.23

CHAPTER 7

NATIONAL LAWS AND THE INTERNATIONAL CONVENTIONS

RIGHTS IN PHONOGRAPHIC AND CINEMATOGRAPHIC RECORDINGS AND WORKS

Preliminary

It should be noted that the statistics and lists of countries in the survey (main text paras. 7.03–7.10) are not updated by this Supplement to reflect the provisions of new laws: these can be identified by reference to the Synopsis of Laws entries (para. 21.00 *et seq.*). 7.02

(3) *The applicable systems*

The Ottoman Law of 1912 has been replaced in Jordan by the Law of April 16, 1992: see paragraph 33.30. 7.05

(7) Duration of protection

7.09 It should be noted that the periods of protection specified in List II (main text para. 20.25) relate to the economic rights of the author. The duration of the moral rights is frequently the same as that of the economic rights (as in the U.K.). In some countries, however, the moral right protection period extends beyond that of the economic rights, and may be perpetual (as in France).

A recent example of a longer period of protection for moral rights is provided by the Russian Federation's Law of July 9, 1993 (see para. 41.10). Under article 28 of the 1993 Law, works that have passed into the public domain (*i.e.* works in respect of which the economic rights have expired 50 years after the author's death) may be used freely, without payment of remuneration, but the rights of attribution and integrity are preserved.

(2) Content of right

(b) Moral rights

7.15 For the French text of the decision of the Cour de Cassation, May 28, 1991, see *RIDA* 149, 197, with comment by Kerever, A. at 161–163. For the English text of the decision, see *IIC* 1992, 702. For comment, see Edelman, B., "Applicable legislation regarding exploitation of colourised United States films in France: the "*John Huston* case" *IIC* 1992, 629.

(b) Broadcasting, cabling and public performance

7.25 *Hotel Rooms (Italy).* For the position as regards reception in hotel rooms, see Fabiani, M. in *Il Diritto di Autore* 1992, 126.

Hotel Rooms (United States). See paragraph 45.90 (e) Public performance.

7.26 (c) **Transborder transmissions.** The principle of the Bogsch theory was further confirmed in the following Austrian cases:

(5) "Direct Satellite Broadcasting II"

(OLG Vienna, June 27, 1991) *GRUR Int.* 1991, 925.

(6) "Direct Satellite Broadcasting III"

(OGH, June 16, 1992) *IIC* 1993, 665.

(5) Exercise of right

(f) *Competition laws*

EEC Treaty: Article 7: Phil Collins case

A joint decision of major importance (referred to herein as *Phil Collins*) in regard to the exercise of intellectual property rights has been given by the European Court of Justice in the cases *Phil Collins v. IMTRAT Handels-GmbH* and *Patricia Im- und Export Verwaltungs-GmbH and Another v. EMI Electrola GmbH* [1993] 3 C.M.L.R. 773, [1994] F.S.R. 166 (ECJ) (French text, *RIDA* 158, 304; German text *GRUR Int.* 1994, 53).

Phil Collins v. IMTRAT concerned a bootleg recording of a performance given by the British performer Phil Collins in the United States. The recording was distributed in Germany, and Phil Collins took action before the Munich Court to stop the marketing and have the records seized.

One of the points at issue was the effect on national law of Article 7(1) of the EEC Treaty, which reads:

> Within the scope of application of this Treaty, and without prejudice to any special provisions contained therein, any discrimination on grounds of nationality shall be prohibited.

Article 125(1) of the German Author's Right Law 1965 provides that German nationals enjoy the protection of the law (including protection against unauthorised copying) for all their performances, irrespective of the place where these are given. With regard to foreign performers, however, protection against unauthorised copying of recordings, and distribution of unauthorised copies, is subject to the fulfilment of certain conditions (performance given in Germany, first publication of legitimate recording in Germany, or protection under State Treaty (art. 125(2)–(5)).

The Phil Collins performance did not satisfy the conditions of article 125 necessary to obtain protection against copying of the recording of that performance, since Phil Collins is a British national, the performance was given in the United States (and hence was not protected under the Rome Convention, the U.S. not being a Member State of the Convention) and the conditions concerning publication were alleged not to have been fulfilled.

If Phil Collins had been a German national, the recording would have been protected against copying (art. 125(1)). The question therefore arose whether German law could validly discriminate between German nationals and other E.C. nationals in this respect.

The Court sought a preliminary ruling from the European Court of Justice on the following questions:

(1) Is copyright law subject to the prohibition of discrimination laid down in Article 7(1) of the EEC Treaty?
(2) If so: does that have the (directly applicable) effect that a Member State which accords protection to its nationals for all their artistic performances, irrespective of the place of performance, also has to accord that protection to nationals of other Member States, or is it compatible with Article 7(1) to attach further conditions (*i.e.* art. 125(2)–(6) of the German Author's Right Law 1965) to granting of protection to nationals of other Member States.

In the *Patricia* case, recordings made by the British performer Cliff Richard were exploited in Germany without the consent of the rightowner (EMI Electrola). The recordings had been made before Germany joined the Rome Convention. The Federal Supreme Court (BGH) referred the following questions to the European Court of Justice:

(1) Is the national copyright law of a Member State subject to the prohibition of discrimination laid down in Article 7(1) EEC?
(2) If so, are the provisions operating in a Member State for the protection of artistic performances (art. 125(1)–(6) of the German Author's Right Law 1965) compatible with Article 7(1) EEC if they do not confer on nationals of another Member State the same standard of protection (national treatment) as they do on national performers?

In its judgment, the European Court of Justice ruled as follows:

(1) Copyright and related rights are within the scope of application of the EEC Treaty within the meaning of Article 7(1); the general principle of non-discrimination laid down by that Article is consequently applicable to those rights.
(2) Article 7(1) EEC must be interpreted as meaning that it prevents the law of a Member State from refusing authors and performing artists of other Member States and their successors in title the right, which is granted by the same law to nationals, to prohibit the marketing in national territory of a phonogram made without their consent, if the performance in question was given outside national territory.

(3) Article 7(1) EEC must be interpreted as meaning that the principle of non-discrimination which it lays down can be relied upon directly before the national court by an author or artist of a Member State or his successor in title in order to seek the protection given to national authors and artists.

Consequently, Article 7(1) EEC prevents Member States from refusing to give authors, performers and film and phonogram producers of other Member States the rights which are granted by the same law to nationals. In the circumstances of the *Phil Collins* case, Germany cannot refuse E.U. Member State performers (*e.g.* from the U.K.) the right to prohibit the marketing in Germany of a phonogram made without their consent, even if the performance was given outside Germany. In other words, E.U. nationals who are authors, performers, film or phonogram producers (or other author's right or related rights owners) are entitled to the same treatment in any European Union Member State as that State gives its own nationals.

For the effect of Article 7 EEC and the *Phil Collins* case on the calculation of duration of term of protection, see paragraph 7.51C.

Collecting Societies

For the general background to *Ministère Public v. Tournier* (reported in [1991] 4 C.M.L.R. 248) see Bertrand, A., "Performing rights societies: the price is right "French-style", or the SACEM cases" [1992] *Ent. L.R.* 146.

General application of Articles 85 and 86 EEC Treaty

Cases concerning the application of Article 85 (prohibition of restrictive practices etc.) and Article 86 (abuse of dominant position) of the EEC Treaty are summarised in Fine, F.L., "The impact of EEC competition law on the music industry" [1992] *Ent. L.R.* 6.

(8) *Non-infringing acts*

For a recent case concerning the application of "fair dealing" (as criticism or review) in relation to broadcasting of extracts from the film *Clockwork Orange*, see *Time Warner Entertainment Co. LP v. Channel Four Television Corp. PLC and Another* [1994] E.M.L.R. 1, summary in [1994] *Ent. L.R.* E–9 (U.K. C.A.), Bradshaw, D., "Fair dealing and the *Clockwork Orange* case: a 'thieves' charter'?" [1994] *Ent. L.R.* 7, and note by Hurst, R.A., in *Copyright World*, December 1993/January 1994, 15.

(9) Remedies and penalties

Civil remedies

7.42 For a case concerning the recognition of the tort of misappropriation as applied to unauthorised copying of sound recordings, see paragraph 45.90, United States: Remedies and penalties.

Penal sanctions

Video tapes held to be documents and thus capable of forgery when produced without the requisite authority and with intention to deceive: unauthorised reproduction also an offence under Law 2387/1920: *Forgery of Videotapes* [1993] F.S.R. 704 (Greece, Areopagus 1990).

Technical measures

Unauthorised making, sale, etc., of satellite signal descramblers may involve breach of copyright and a criminal offence: *U.S. v. Hux* 19 USPQ 2d 1541 (U.S.C.A. 8, 1991).

Circulation, export and transit of counterfeit and pirated goods

EEC Council Regulation No. 3842/86 of December 1, 1986 deals with the prohibition of release for free circulation of counterfeit goods. The E.C. Commission has submitted a proposal (COM (93) 329 final of August 16, 1993, [1993] O.J. C238/9) for a Council Regulation laying down measures to prohibit the release for free circulation, export or transit of counterfeit and pirated goods: see *WIPR* 1994, 68.

(3) *The Rome Convention*

Chile

7.46 The phonogram producer now has a statutory right to 50 per cent. of the remuneration. See paragraph 25.90.

Czechoslovakia

The entitlement of performers and producers to remuneration continues in the Czech Republic and the Slovak Republic. See paras. 27.70, 42.65.

Accordingly, the reference to Czechoslovakia should be deleted, and the Czech Republic and the Slovak Republic inserted in the list, with the reference "performers and producers".

Greece

Add to the list on pp. 299–300 in the main text: "Greece: performers and producers". See paragraph 30.50.

Ireland

It will be necessary to introduce a specific remuneration right for performers, as in the United Kingdom (see below); following the adoption of E.C. Directive 92/100.

Netherlands

Add to list on pp. 299–300 in the main text: "Netherlands: performers and producers". See paragraph 37.70.

United Kingdom

Following the adoption of E.C. Community Directive 92/100 (see para. 7.51A), performers will have an independent right to remuneration for the broadcasting and public communication of sound recordings in the United Kingdom. It remains to be seen how the United Kingdom law is to be amended to put the Directive into effect, and how this will affect the present voluntary sharing arrangements.

Rights of broadcasting organisations.

For the Rome Convention revisions sought by the European Broadcasting Union, see Rumphorst, W., "Protection of broadcasting organisations under the Rome Convention", *UNESCO Cop. Bull.* 1993, XXVII/2/10 and Opinion in [1992] *EIPR* 339.

(4) *The Phonograms Convention*

Content of right

Correction. In the main text, the words "or distribution" should be added after "importation".

(6) *Other Conventions, Treaties and Agreements*

(c) Audiovisual Works Registration Treaty 1989

7.49 The following countries, in addition to those named in the main text, have become parties to the Treaty (see *Copyright* 1994, 14):

>Argentina (from July 29, 1992); Brazil (from June 26, 1993); Chile (from December 29, 1993); Czech Republic (from January 1, 1993); Senegal (from April 3, 1994); Slovak Republic (from January 1, 1993).

The Registry was opened on September 1, 1991: see *Copyright* 1992, 83.

Correction. The date of the Audiovisual Works Registration Treaty is 1989, not 1988, as indicated by heading (c) on p. 303 in the main text.

(7) *Other instruments and developments*

(i) Council of Europe

7.50 (7) Recommendation No. R(91)14 of September 27, 1991, on the legal protection of encrypted television services.

European Convention relating to questions on copyright law and neighbouring rights in the framework of transfrontier broadcasting by satellite ("The Transfrontier Satellite Broadcasting Convention")

The Transfrontier Satellite Broadcasting Convention was adopted on February 16, 1994, by the Committee of Ministers of the Council of Europe. The Convention will be opened for signature on May 11, 1994. The following is a short summary of some of the main provisions of the Convention.

The Convention provides that a transmission by direct broadcasting satellite of works and other contributions occurs in the State Party in the territory of which the transmission originates, and therefore shall be governed exclusively by the law of that State (Art. 3(1)).

The State Party in the territory of which the transmission originates means the State Party in which the programme-carrying signals transmitted by satellite are introduced, under the control and responsibility of the broadcasting organisation, into an uninterrupted chain of communication via the up-link and down to the earth (Art. 3(2)).

Article 3(3) deals with transmissions originating in States which are not parties to the Convention (where there is no level of protection equivalent to that of the Convention and where the up-link is from a State Party) and where the responsible broadcasting organisation is situated in a State Party: in these cases the transmission is deemed to originate in the State Party concerned.

Article 4(1) provides that authors of works mentioned in Article 2 of the Berne Convention shall, as far as transfrontier broadcasting by satellite is concerned, be protected in conformity with the provisions of the Convention (Paris text 1971). In particular, rights for transfrontier broadcasting by satellite concerning such works shall be acquired contractually.

Article 4(2) provides for the preservation of certain existing collective agreements (excluding application to cinematographic works).

Article 5 deals with the protection of neighbouring rights in accordance with the provisions of the Rome Convention: a State Party is not to avail itself of the faculty provided by Article 19 of the Convention (see main text para. 4.31). Article 5(4) establishes the principle of payment of remuneration to performers and phonogram producers when commercially published phonograms are used for transfrontier broadcasting by satellite.

The simultaneous, complete and unchanged retransmission by terrestrial means of broadcasts by satellite is not, as such, covered by the Convention (Art. 6).

In their mutual relations, Parties which are members of the E.C. are to apply Community rules and are not therefore to apply the rules arising from the Convention, except in so far as there is no Community rule governing the particular subject concerned (Art. 9(1)).

The Convention will enter into force three months after the date on which seven States, of which at least five are Member States of the Council of Europe, have expressed consent to be bound by the Convention.

The provisions of the Convention should be compared with those of the E.C. Directive on Satellite Broadcasting and Cable Retransmission: see paragraph 7.51B.

Declaration on neighbouring rights. On February 16, 1994 the Committee of Ministers made a declaration concerning the need for a general improvement in the protection of neighbouring rights, and proposed continued examination of the subject. The Committee considered that priority should be given to the study of, *inter alia*, rights of performers, phonogram producers and broadcasting organisations with regard to cable retransmission, the right of performers and phonogram producers to authorise reproduction of their performances and phonograms, moral rights of performers and the duration of protection of rightowners.

(ii) EEC

(References are now made to the European Union ("E.U."), rather than the European Economic Community.)

7.51 **A. Directives.** The following Directives have been issued since May 14, 1991:

(1) Council Directive of November 19, 1992, on rental and lending rights, and certain rights related to copyright (Directive 92/100/EEC) ("The Rental and Related Rights Directive") (see para. 7.51A).
(2) Council Directive of September 27, 1993, on copyright and rights related to copyright applicable to satellite broadcasting and cable retransmission (Directive 93/83/EEC) ("The Satellite Broadcasting and Cable Retransmission Directive") (see para. 7.51B).
(3) Council Directive, of October 29, 1993, harmonising the term of protection of copyright and certain related rights (Directive 93/98/EEC) ("The Term Directive") (see para. 7.51C).

The following is a brief summary of some of the principal points of these Directives.

1. The Rental and Related Rights Directive

7.51A The Rental and Related Rights Directive deals mainly with two distinct matters, namely rental and lending rights (Chapter I) and rights related to copyright (Chapter II).

Rental and lending rights

Member States must grant exclusive rental and lending rights as regards copyright works and other subject matter (Art. 1(1)).

Article 1(2) defines "rental" as "making available for use, for a limited period of time and for direct or indirect economic or commercial advantage". "Lending" means making available for use, for a limited period of time and not for direct or indirect economic or commercial advantage, when it is made through establishments which are accessible to the public (Art. 1(3)). Thus, broadly, "rental" has the element of a commercial transaction, and "lending" of a non-commercial loan to a member of the public.

The exhaustion principle does not apply to rental or lending (Art. 1(4)).
The exclusive rights of rental and lending belong to:
— the author in respect of the original and copies of his work;
— the performer in respect of fixations of his performance;
— the phonogram producer in respect of his phonograms;
— the producer of the first fixation of a film ("the film first fixation producer") in respect of the original and copies of his film.
(Art. 2(1))

Authors of films

The principal director of a cinematographic or audiovisual work is, for the purposes of the Directive, to be considered as its author or one of its authors: Member States may provide for others to be considered as its co-authors (Art. 2(2): *cf.* Art. 2(1) of the Term Directive (see para. 7.51C)).

Transfer of rights

The rental and lending rights may be transferred (Art. 2(4)).

Article 2(5) provides that (without prejudice to Art. 2(7), see below) when a contract concerning film production is concluded by performers with a film producer, the performer shall be presumed, subject to contractual clauses to the contrary, to have transferred his rental right, subject to a right of equitable remuneration (Art. 4).

Where an author or performer has transferred his rental right concerning a phonogram or film to a producer, he retains the right to obtain an equitable remuneration for the rental: this right is unwaivable (Art. 4(1)(2)).

Rights related to copyright

The provisions of Chapter II of the Directive are in many respects similar to those of Articles 7, 10, 12 and 13 of the Rome Convention (see main text para. 7.46). In a number of aspects, however, the Directive provides for greater protection than that afforded by the Rome Convention, and the following are instances which may be noted in this connection:

(a) performers, phonogram producers and first film fixation producers (as well as authors) are granted rental and lending rights (under Chapter I);

(b) first film fixation producers are granted related rights, whereas such producers are not protected under the Rome Convention;
(c) originated cable transmissions are protected under the Directive, whereas the Rome Convention only protects broadcasts by wireless means (see definition, Rome Convention, Art. 3(f));
(d) performers and phonogram producers are granted an equitable remuneration right in respect of the use of commercially published phonograms for wireless broadcasting or communication to the public, and States must grant this right, whereas under the Rome Convention the right can be excluded or limited by a reservation under Article 16: furthermore, it would seem that the right applies whether the use is direct or indirect, whereas under the Rome Convention, the use must be direct for the right to arise;
(e) performers, phonogram producers, film first fixation producers and broadcasting organisations are granted a distribution right, whereas the Rome Convention does not grant such a right.

While the Directive, as adopted, incorporated the Rome Convention minima of 20 years' protection for related rights, this has been replaced by the 50 year period established by the Term Directive, so in this respect, the resulting term of protection under Community law is superior to that under the Rome Convention (or, for that matter, the Berne Convention, see para. 7.51C).

Broadcasting and communication to the public

Article 8(2) of the Directive establishes a remuneration right in respect of the use of commercially published phonograms for "broadcasting by wireless means or for any communication to the public". Articles 11 and 11*bis* of the Berne Convention (Paris text 1971) refer to "communication to the public" and this phrase, in the context of the Berne Convention, covers cabling. However, it would appear that Article 8(2) of the Directive does not cover cabling, since "broadcasts" may be transmitted by wire or over the air (Directive, Art. 6), whereas Article 8(2) of the Directive refers to "broadcasting by wireless means" (see note below under heading, Bibliography). Member States may nevertheless grant greater rights than those afforded by Article 8(2) and thus extend the remuneration right to cabling.

Performers

Member States must provide the following rights for performers:

(1) to authorise or prohibit the fixation of their performances (Art. 6(1));

The Rental and Related Rights Directive 7.51A

(2) to authorise or prohibit the direct or indirect reproduction of fixations of their performances (Art. 7(1));

(3) to authorise or prohibit the broadcasting by wireless means and the communication to the public of their performances, except where the performance is itself already a broadcast performance or is made from a fixation (Art. 8(1));

(4) to a share of the equitable remuneration paid for the broadcasting by wireless means or communication to the public of commercially published phonograms (Art. 8(2));

(5) to distribute to the public copies of fixations of their performances (subject to Community exhaustion) (see main text, para. 7.51) (Art. 9(1)(2)).

Phonogram producers

Member States must provide the following rights for phonogram producers:

(1) to authorise or prohibit the direct or indirect reproduction of their phonograms (Art. 7(1));

(2) to a share of the equitable remuneration paid for the broadcasting by wireless means or communication to the public of commercially published phonograms (Art. 8(2));

(3) to distribute to the public copies of their phonograms (subject to Community exhaustion) (Art. 9(1)(2)).

Film first fixation producers

Member States must provide the following rights for film first fixation producers:

(1) to authorise or prohibit the direct or indirect reproduction of their films (Art. 7(1));

(2) to distribute to the public copies of their films (subject to Community exhaustion) (Art. 9(1)(2)).

Broadcasting organisations

Member States must provide the following rights for broadcasting organisations:

(1) to authorise or prohibit the fixation of their broadcasts (Art. 6(1));

(2) to authorise or prohibit the direct or indirect reproduction of fixations of their broadcasts (Art. 7(1));

(3) to distribute to the public copies of fixations of their broadcasts (subject to Community exhaustion) (Art. 9(1)(2)).

Duration

The duration of protection is governed by the Term Directive (see para. 7.51C).

Application in time

Article 13(1) provides that the Directive shall apply to all copyright works, performances, phonograms, broadcasts and film first fixations still protected in Member States on July 1, 1994, by Member States' legislation or "the criteria for protection under the provisions of this Directive". What those criteria are remains to be clarified.

In general the Directive must be brought into force in the legislation of Member States by July 1, 1994, but there are special provisions concerning existing films, the recognition of directors as authors, etc. (Arts. 13 and 15).

Bibliography

For a detailed study of the Directive, with text of and comments on each Article, see Reinbothe, J. and von Lewinski, S., *The E.C. Directive on Rental and Lending Rights and on Piracy* (Sweet & Maxwell, 1993): as to cabling see pp. 94–97.

See also Reinbothe, J. and von Lewinski, S., "The E.C. Rental Directive one year after its adoption: some selected issues" [1993] *Ent. L.R.* 169.

2. The Satellite Broadcasting and Cable Retransmission Directive

Satellite Broadcasting

7.51B The Satellite Broadcasting and Cable Retransmission Directive defines "communication to the public by satellite" as

> the act of introducing, under the control and responsibility of the broadcasting organisation, the programme-carrying signals intended for reception by the public into an uninterrupted chain of communication leading to the satellite and down towards the earth.

(Art. 1(2)(a)).

The Satellite Broadcasting and Cable Retransmission Directive 7.51B

The act of communication to the public by satellite occurs solely in the Member State where, under the control and responsibility of the broadcasting organisation, the programme-carrying signals are introduced into an uninterrupted chain of communication leading to the satellite and down towards the earth (Art. 1(2)(b)).

Member States must provide an exclusive right to the author to authorise the communication to the public by satellite of copyright works, subject to the provisions of the Directive (Art. 2).

Thus the Directive adopts an approach related to the "emission theory", rather than the "communication theory" based on the Bogsch theory (see main text para. 4.63). Nevertheless it is important to note that the Directive does not apply to broadcasts originating outside the European Union. Thus, in the case of France, where the principle of the Bogsch theory is accepted in the jurisprudence, the permission of the local rightowner will still be necessary in the case of satellite broadcasts where the act of communication to the French public (in terms of the Directive) takes place, say, in the United States. Similarly, if and when Austria becomes bound by the Directive, the Austrian Courts will be able to continue to apply the Bogsch theory in respect of satellite broadcasts originating outside the territory composed of Member States of the European Union, and directed to Austria (see main text paras. 4.63, 7.54).

Where an act of communication to the public by satellite occurs in a non-Community State which does not provide the level of protection provided by the Directive:

(a) if the programme-carrying signals are transmitted to the satellite from an up-link station situated in a Member State, the act of communication is deemed to have occurred in that Member State; or
(b) if there is no use of an up-link station situated in a Member State, but a broadcasting organisation in a Member State has commissioned the act of communication, that act is deemed to have occurred in that Member State. (Art. 1(2)(d)).

Compulsory licences are excluded (Art. 3(1)).

The rights of performers, phonogram producers and broadcasting organisations under the Rental and Related Rights Directive are maintained in respect of communication to the public by satellite (Art. 4).

Transitional provisions regulate the validity of existing agreements, which are subject to the provisions of Articles 1(2), 2 and 3 from January 1, 2000.

Cable retransmission

Member States must ensure that when programmes from other Member States are retransmitted by cable in their territory, the applicable copyright and related rights are observed and that such retransmission takes place on the basis of individual or collective contractual agreements between copyright owners, holders of related rights and cable operators. However, already established statutory licence systems may continue to operate until December 31, 1997 (Art. 8).

Cable retransmission rights are to be exercised through a collecting society (except as regards the rights of broadcasting organisations) (Arts. 9 and 10).

There are provisions for mediation where no agreement is reached regarding authorisation of cable retransmission of a broadcast (Art. 11), and concerning prevention of abuse of any negotiation position (Art. 12).

The laws of Member States must comply with the Directive by January 1, 1995 (Art. 14(1)).

For a survey of the problems considered in the formulation of the Directive, see Kern, Ph., "The E.C. 'Common Position' on copyright applicable to satellite broadcasting and cable retransmission" [1993] *EIPR* 276.

3. The Term Directive

7.51C The Term Directive provides for the institution of the following protection periods in the laws of all Member States, in so far as not already subsisting:

(a) *Rights of authors of literary or artistic works:* life plus 70 years p.m.a. (Art. 1).

(b) *Cinematographic or audiovisual works:* the term of protection expires 70 years after the death of the last of the following persons to survive, whether or not these persons are designated as co-authors (*i.e.* under the laws of the respective Member States): the principal director, the author of the screenplay, the author of the dialogue and the composer of specially created music (Art. 2(2)).

(c) *Rights of performers:* 50 years from the date of the performances, but if published or lawfully communicated to the public within this period, then 50 years from the date of the first such publication or the first such communication, whichever is the earlier (Art. 3(1)).

(d) *Rights of phonogram producers:* 50 years from fixation, but if the phonogram is lawfully published or lawfully communicated to the public during this period, the rights expire 50 years from the date of the first such publication or the first such communication, whichever is the earlier (Art. 3(2)).
(e) *Rights of film first fixation producers:* 50 years from fixation, but if the film is lawfully published or lawfully communicated to the public during this period, the rights expire 50 years from the date of the first such publication or the first such communication, whichever is the earlier (Art. 3(3)).
(f) *Rights of broadcasting organisations*: 50 years from first transmission of the broadcast (whether by wire or cable, or over air, including by satellite or cable (Art. 3(4)).

Authorship of cinematographic and audiovisual works

Member States must provide that the principal director of a cinematographic or audiovisual work shall be considered as its author or one of its authors: Member States are free to designate other co-authors (Art. 2(1)). Member States need not introduce this provision before July 1, 1997 (Art. 10(5)). States may choose not to apply this provision to cinematographic or audiovisual works created before July 1, 1994 (Art. 10(4)).

This provision, together with the rule for calculating term of protection in film works (Art. 2(2)), may lead to complications and practical difficulties. There will be no consistency in the European Union as to the persons who are considered authors of film works. In Ireland and the United Kingdom, where the maker alone is at present recognised as the film work rightowner, it will be necessary to introduce legislation adding the principal director as an author (Art. 2(1)). In France certain individuals are recognised as film work authors who are not so recognised in Germany (see main text paras. 6.26, 6.33).

This disparity of provisions throughout the Member States will mean that in this respect there will be little improvement on the present situation: that is, permissions for film use in copying, broadcasting or cable retransmission will need to be sought from different classes of persons in the different Member States, in so far as the required permission is not obtainable through a collecting society.

Protection of works originating in third countries: comparison of terms

Article 7 provides that where the country of origin of the work (*i.e.* in the case of works, country of author's nationality, or place of first publication) is a third country (*i.e.* a country outside the E.U.) and the author of the work is not a Community national, the term of protection granted by Member States expires on the date of expiry of protection of the work in the country of origin (but in any case the terms cannot exceed those laid down in the Directive).

In most countries of the Berne Union, the term of protection is 50 years p.m.a. Works originating in these countries will therefore only enjoy protection for 50 years p.m.a. in the European Union.

The comparison of terms principle is itself enshrined in the Berne Convention (Paris text 1971, Art. 7(8)), but up to the present it has mainly operated to shorten the term of protection of works originating outside the Berne Union. Now, with the European Union States applying the 70 year p.m.a. term, the basic term of 50 years p.m.a. guaranteed by the Berne Convention (Paris text 1971, Art. 7(1)) will need to be upgraded in the laws of third countries, if works originating in such countries are to enjoy the full term of protection in the European Union.

Related rights

Article 7(2) provides that the terms of protection for related rights (as laid down in Art. 3), shall also apply to rightholders who are not Community nationals, provided Member States grant them protection. However, the comparison of terms is applicable.

Moral rights

The term of protection of moral rights is not regulated by the Directive (Art. 9).

Protection of existing works

While it is clear that the term of protection of newly produced works and subject matter is regulated by the Directive, the situation as regards the term of protection of works existing on July 1, 1995 (when the Directive comes into operation) presents complexities and problems which are yet to be resolved.

Article 10(2) provides that the terms of protection provided for in the Directive shall apply to all works and subject matter which are protected in at least one Member State on July 1, 1995.

Certain European Union States grant a period of protection longer than 50 years p.m.a. (Germany 70 years p.m.a., Greece 70 years p.m.a. Spain 60 years p.m.a., France 70 years p.m.a. for musical works).

Considering the position as at July 1, 1995, and taking the United Kingdom (50 years p.m.a. protection period) and Germany as examples, the following cases are among those affected by Article 10(2) of the Directive:

(a) A work in its 45th year p.m.a. of protection in the United Kingdom will continue to be protected throughout the European Union until the 70th year p.m.a.: thus it will have its period of protection extended.
(b) A work in its 65th year p.m.a. of protection in Germany will be protected throughout the European Union for another five years, and will thus come back into protection in European Union States where the protection for that work had previously expired.

One of the vital questions will thus be: which works will be protected in Germany on July 1, 1995?

Germany applies the comparison of terms test, so that (subject to the principle of the decision in the *Phil Collins* case, see para. 7.38) works having a foreign country of origin where protection has expired will not be protected in Germany on July 1, 1995.

The provisions of Article 10 apply equally to performances, phonograms, film first fixations and broadcasts, so that, for example, a phonogram protected in Germany on July 1, 1995 will be protected throughout the European Union for the balance of the 50 year term, even though protection had previously expired in, for example, Italy.

Under the German Author's Right Law 1965:

(a) German nationals enjoy protection in Germany for their unpublished works, and for their published works, wherever published (art. 120(1)).
(b) German nationals enjoy protection in Germany for all their performances, wherever these took place (art. 125(1)).
(c) German nationals or companies enjoy protection in Germany for all their unpublished phonograms and for their published phonograms, wherever published (art. 126(1)).
(d) German broadcasting organisations enjoy protection in Germany for their broadcasts, wherever these are transmitted (art. 127(1)).

By virtue of the provisions of Article 7 of the EEC Treaty, as applied in the *Phil Collins* case, Germany is obliged to grant protection on the basis that "E.U." is substituted for "German" in (a)-(d) above.

This being the case, it would appear that many works, performances, phonograms, film first fixations and broadcasts originating in other European Union States will be protected in Germany on July 1, 1995, even though they may not be protected in their country of origin, and even though Germany, had it been able to apply the comparison of terms test, would not otherwise protect such works or subject matter.

It is anticipated that before July 1, 1995 there will be extensive studies of this question, and indications from the European Union Commission as to its views on the interpretation of Article 10(2), and how it should be put into effect.

See Dworkin, G. and Sterling, J.A.L., "Phil Collins and the Term Directive" [1994] *EIPR* 187.

Previous exploitation

Article 10(3) provides that the Directive shall be without prejudice to any acts of exploitation performed before July 1, 1995.

Compliance with the Directive

Member States must bring into force before July 1, 1995 the laws and provisions necessary to comply with Articles 1 to 11 of the Directive.

7.51D **B. Working Programme** The current position as to the Working Programme items listed in the main text is as follows:

(1) *Proposal on rental right, lending right and related rights*: Directive now adopted (92/100/EEC, see para. 7.51A).
(2) *Proposal requiring membership of the Berne and Rome Conventions*: Alternative Council Resolution recommending membership adopted May 14, 1992 ([1992] O.J. C138/1).
(3) *Proposal concerning private copying*: Consultation Document issued by Directorate General XV in September 1993, with invitation to interested parties to communicate their comments: no proposed Directive yet published.
(4) *Proposal on protection of databases*: Amended proposal of November 15, 1993 ([1993] O.J. C308/1) under discussion.
(5) *Proposal on term of protection*: Directive now adopted (93/98/EEC, see para. 7.51C).
(6) *Proposal on satellite broadcasting and cable retransmission*: Directive now adopted (93/83/EEC, see para. 7.51B).

Moral rights

Discussions are proceeding on the question of harmonisation of protection of moral rights.

Bibliography

A Table of E.C. Intellectual Property Measures, giving the current position on Commission proposals and their status, is published monthly in *European Intellectual Property Review*. For the background, see Silvestro, A., "Towards E.C. harmonisation of the term of protection of copyright and so-called 'related' rights" [1993] *Ent. L.R.* 73.

(iii) GATT

Following the conclusion of the Uruguay Round of Multilaterial Trade Negotiations on December 15, 1993, the Final Act embodying the results of the negotiations, including the annexed Agreement on Trade-Related Aspects of Intellectual Property Rights (TRIPs), was signed at the Marrakech Ministerial Meeting in Spring, 1994. The following is a brief listing of some of the main provisions of the TRIPs Agreement ("Members" denotes Contracting States). It is anticipated that a period of time will follow the Marrakech meeting before the Agreement is in force between those States which accept it. 7.52

Article 1. Members must give national treatment to the nationals of other Members.

Article 2. Obligations under the Intellectual Property Conventions are preserved.

Article 3. Scope and definition of national treatment.

Article 4. Application of principle of most-favoured national treatment.

Article 9. Members shall comply with Articles 1 to 21 and Appendix of the Berne Convention (Paris text 1971) (exception concerning Article 6*bis*, moral rights).

Article 10. Computer programs are to be protected as literary works under the Berne Convention 1971; data compilations constituting intellectual creations are also to be protected.

Article 11. Rental rights (with certain exceptions) are to be granted in respect of computer programs and cinematographic works.

Article 12. The basic term of protection is 50 years p.m.a.

Article 14. Performers, phonogram producers and broadcasting organisations are to have rights similar to those granted under Articles 7, 10 and 13, respectively, of the Rome Convention. Rental rights of phonogram producers are to be instituted or maintained. The basic term of protection for performers and phonogram producers is 50 years, and that for broadcasting organisations, 20 years.

Articles 15–21. Protection of trademarks.

Articles 22–26. Protection of geographical indications.

Articles 27–34. Protection of patents.

Articles 35–38. Protection of semiconductor topographies.

Article 39. Protection of trade secrets.

Article 40. Control of anti-competitive practices in contractual licences.

Articles 41–61. Enforcement of intellectual property rights, including civil and administrative procedures and remedies, border measures and criminal procedures.

Article 62. Acquisition and maintenance of intellectual property rights and related *inter partes* procedures.

Articles 63–64. Dispute prevention and settlement.

Articles 65–67. Transitional arrangements.

Articles 68–73. Institutional arrangements: final provisions.

Note. As to questions of retroactivity arising under Article 18 of the Berne Convention 1971, in the context of the United States, see paragraph 45.90, (g) Convention Membership.

7.53   *(iv) WIPO*

(a) Possible Protocol to the Berne Convention

The following meetings of the Committee of Experts on a possible Protocol to the Berne Convention have taken place in the period November 1991 to

The Term Directive 7.53

January 1994. The documentation published in *Copyright* is noted under the respective Sessions.

(1) *First Session:* Geneva, November 4–8, 1991. Documentation: "Questions concerning a possible Protocol to the Berne Convention: Part I, Memorandum" (*Copyright* 1992, 30); Report (*Copyright* 1992, 40).

(2) *Second Session:* Geneva, February 10–18, 1992. Documentation: "Questions concerning a possible Protocol to the Berne Convention: Part II, Memorandum" (*Copyright* 1992, 66); Report (Copyright 1992, 95).

(3) *Third Session:* Geneva, June 21–25, 1993. Documentation: "Preparatory document, Part I, Introduction" (*Copyright* 1993, 72); Part III—New Items (*Copyright* 1993, 84).

See also the document prepared for the Thirteenth Session (Third extraordinary) of the Assembly of the Berne Union, *Copyright* 1992, 182.

Among the matters discussed at the meetings (in addition to those mentioned in main text para. 7.53) were (a) author's right of reproduction, including storage of works in computer systems, (b) private reproduction for personal use, (c) rental and public lending rights, (d) distribution and importation rights, (e) communication to the public by satellite broadcasting, (f) non-voluntary broadcasting licences, (g) term of protection, (h) national treatment (including the questions of application in the case of public lending right, and of collective administration, in relation to payments for cultural and social purposes).

A fourth Session is planned for December 1994.

(b) Possible Instrument on the Protection of the Rights of Performers and Producers of Phonograms

It was originally proposed that protection for producers of phonograms should be included in the proposed Protocol to the Berne Convention (see First Session Memorandum, paras. 56–69, *Copyright* 1992, 38). Opinions were divided as to whether sound recordings should be included in the Berne Convention. It was decided that a separate Committee of Experts should consider the protection of producers of sound recordings, and WIPO prepared a Draft Model Law for consideration (see below). It was subsequently decided to extend the scope of the possible new instrument to cover the rights of performers. The following Expert Committee Meetings have taken place in this connection.

(1) Committee of Experts on a WIPO Model Law on the Protection of Producers of Sound Recordings, Geneva, June 15–19, 1992. Documentation: Draft WIPO Model Law (*Copyright* 1992, 152); Report (*Copyright* 1992, 188).
(2) Committee of Experts on a Possible Instrument on the Protection of the Rights of Performers and Producers of Phonograms.
  (a) *First Session*: Geneva, June 28–July 2, 1993. Documentation: Preparatory Document (*Copyright* 1993, 142); Report (*Copyright* 1993, 196).
  (b) *Second Session*: Geneva, November 8–12, 1993. Documentation: Report (*Copyright* 1994, 44).

The matters discussed at the meetings include, in addition to a general consideration of the rights to be accorded to performers and phonogram producers: (a) remuneration for private copying, (b) distribution and importation rights, (c) rental and public lending rights, (d) adaptation rights, (e) rights of communication to the public and public performance, (f) moral rights of performers, (g) exercise and transfer of economic rights, (h) national treatment, (i) term of protection, and (j) collective administration of rights.

Among the matters which were extensively discussed was the question of the possibility of an establishment of an exclusive right of communication to the public for both performers and phonogram producers.

One of the notable declarations was that made by the Delegation of the United States of America that the time had come to bring the protection of phonogram producers and performers in line with that of other creators protected under the Berne Convention: a lower level of protection should not be granted to one class of creative artists (Report, para. 9). This view would seem to accord in principle with that expressed in main text paragraph 6.15, namely that the category of phonographic work should be recognised as a separate and distinct subject of protection by copyright and author's right, where the phonographic production results from creative input.

A third Session is planned for December 1994.

(v) EEA Agreement

7.54 The European Economic Area Agreement 1992 regulates relations between the EFTA countries (Austria, Finland, Iceland, Liechtenstein, Norway and Sweden, but not Switzerland, which has not accepted the Agreement) and the European Union. The implementation of the Agreement remains to be effected (see [1994] O.J. L1/546). Protocol 28 of the Agreement deals with intellectual property and provides, *inter alia*, that the EFTA States will adjust their legislation on intellectual property in order to reach at least the level of protection of intellectual property prevailing in the Community on signature of the Agreement. The "Community exhaustion principle" (see main text para. 7.51) is to be implemented in all Contracting States.

The effect of Article 65(2) of, and Annex XVII to the Agreement is that, *inter alia*, the provisions of the E.C. Directives on the protection of semiconductor topographies and computer programs (see main text para. 7.51) will come into effect in the Contracting States of EFTA. Possibly the Directives on rental and related rights, satellite and cable retransmission and term (see para. 7.51) will be similarly applied. (For the procedure in this respect see [1994] O.J. L1/546.)

The EEA Agreement has to a certain extent been overtaken by the agreement (March 1994) that (subject to the respective notifications) Austria, Finland, Norway and Sweden will join the European Union.

The net result will be that the principles of E.C. copyright legislation, and the provisions of the respective Directives, will apply throughout the European Union and the affected EFTA countries. This represents a formidable body of precedent for the rest of the world, and with the application of rules of material reciprocity as regards third countries, will doubtless affect the content of intellectual property legislation throughout the world.

For a general survey, see Brown J. and Robert G., Opinion in [1992] *EIPR* 379.

(vi) North American Free Trade Agreement (NAFTA) 7.55

The North American Free Trade Agreement, 1992 (between Canada, Mexico and the United States) contains extensive provisions concerning intellectual property, of which the following is a brief summary.

Article 1701. Adequate and effective protection and enforcement of intellectual property rights to be provided by each Party: provisions of (*inter alia*) Berne Convention (Paris text 1971) and Phonograms Convention to be given effect.

Article 1703. National treatment to be accorded by each Party to nationals of the other Parties, including phonogram producers and performers, with possibility of material reciprocity as regards exercise of phonogram performing (secondary) rights. No formalities allowed as condition of protection.

Article 1704. Control of abusive or anti-competitive practices or conditions.

Article 1705. Each Party to protect works covered by Article 2 of the Berne Convention, and any other original works, including computer programs and databases (where selection or arrangement of contents constitutes an intellectual creation). Berne Convention rights (*e.g.* Art. 9 (reproduction)), plus rights of importation, first public distribution and rental to be granted to authors. Term of protection (other than for photographs and works of applied art): basic minimum of 50 years where term not calculated on life of author. Possibility of introducing limitations or exceptions (on the lines of Art. 9(2) of the Berne Convention 1971).

Article 1706. Producers of sound recordings to have the right to authorise or prohibit reproduction, importation of unauthorised copies, distribution and rental. Basic term of protection: 50 years from making. Limitations and exceptions provisions as under Article 1705.

Article 1707. Protection of encrypted programme-carrying satellite signals (criminal and civil remedies).

Article 1708. Protection of trademarks.

Article 1709. Protection of patents.

Article 1710. Protection of semiconductor topographies.

Article 1712. Protection of geographical indications.

Article 1713. Protection of industrial designs.

Articles 1715–1717. Procedures and civil and criminal remedies, penalties.

Article 1718. Border enforcement.

Article 1719. Cooperation and technical assistance.

Article 1720. Protection of existing subject matter (in general, the principles of Art. 18 of the Berne Convention 1971 apply).

Article 1721. Definitions (including "encrypted programme-carrying satellite signal", "intellectual property rights", "nationals of another Party", "public").

Annex 1701.3. Accession to intellectual property Conventions.

Annex 1705.7. Protection in the United States of public domain motion pictures produced in another Party's territory. See Komen, E., "NAFTA's copyright magic show: retroactive protection for films does a disappearing act" *Copyright World* 1994, February, 44.

Note. As to questions of retroactivity arising under Article 18 of the Berne Convention 1971, in the context of United States law, see paragraph 45.90, (g) Convention membership.

(vii) Asian Pacific Economic Cooperation Forum (APEC)

The recently formed Asian Pacific Economic Co-operation Forum deals with trading relations among nations bordering the Pacific Ocean. It may be anticipated that the recognition of intellectual property rights will be on the agenda of future meetings of the Forum.   7.56

APPENDIX A

THE RECORD PERFORMING RIGHT: HISTORICAL BACKGROUND

(4) *Switzerland*

The record performing right is now recognised in Switzerland (Law of October 9, 1992, art. 35(1)). See paragraph 43.70.   7A.05

The International Convention

Rome Convention 1961, Article 12

The position in Luxembourg and the Netherlands, among the countries which voted against Article 12 at the 1961 Conference, has changed.   7A.10

Luxembourg is now obliged to introduce the principle of Article 12 by virtue of the E.C. Directive 92/100 on Rental and Lending Rights and Related Rights, while the Netherlands has adopted a new law in this connection, incorporating the principle of Article 12 (see paras. 35.00, 37.00).

Of the countries which abstained from voting on Article 12:

(1) Denmark, Finland, Norway, Spain and Sweden recognise the principle of Article 12 in their respective laws, as mentioned in the main text.

(2) Portugal (see main text para. 40.40), Belgium, since 1991 (see para. 23.30) and Switzerland (see para. 43.70) incorporate the principle of Article 12 in their respective laws.

Thus, of the countries which voted against, or abstained from voting on Article 12, the only ones which, apart from Yugoslavia, have not yet introduced the principle of the Article in their laws are Monaco, South Africa, Tunisia and the United States.

APPENDIX B

PERFORMERS' RIGHTS

Introductory

7B.01 In consulting main text paragraphs 7B.21, 7B.22, note the special position of the Isle of Man: see paragraph 32.70.

General and specific rights

United States

7B.04 For a recent survey see Goodenough, O.R., "The price of fame: the development of the right of publicity in the United States" [1992] *EIPR* 55, 90.

(b) *Rome Convention*

The following additional States have become parties to the Rome Convention: Argentina, Australia, Bolivia, Czech Republic, Greece, Jamaica, the Netherlands, Nigeria, Slovak Republic, Switzerland.
See Table A, Addendum, paragraph 20.11.

7B.07

Ownership and exercise of rights

Consent of performer

For a United Kingdom case as to performer's consent, see *Mad Hat Music Ltd. v. Pulse Eight Records Ltd.* [1993] E.M.L.R. 172, note in [1992] *Ent. L.R.* E-79 (Ch.D., Mervyn Davies J., 1992).

7B.16

Remedies and penalties

See Sherrard, B.G., "Performers' protection: the evolution of a complete offence" [1992] *Ent. L.R.* 57.

7B.20

LISTINGS OF NATIONAL LAWS (PERFORMERS' RIGHTS)

The following amendments result from the new legislation noted in the Synopsis of Laws (see para. 21.00 *et seq.*).

7B.21

E.U. Member States

E.U. Member States will be required, as from July 1, 1994, to have legislation granting the necessary level of protection to performers in accordance with E.C. Directive 92/100 (see paras. 7.51A, 20.20). The E.U. Member States regarding which notice of the relevant legislation on the level of protection for performers had not been received as at January 1, 1994, are Belgium, Ireland, Luxembourg and the United Kingdom. Since protection of performers may be granted at Level I, Ix, II or IIx in accordance with the Directive, and since it is not known which particular level will be ascribed in the legislation of these four States, they are not included in the following lists, but the fact that protection will be granted at one of these levels should be noted. Furthermore, upon implementation of the new legislation, it will be necessary to delete Ireland, Luxembourg and the United Kingdom from the Level IV listing in the main text.

(1) Levels of protection (Performers' rights)

Level I

Add
Bolivia (para. 23.80)
Bulgaria (para. 24.70)
Czech Republic (para. 27.70)
Estonia (para. 28.60)
Finland (para. 29.20)
Jordan (para. 33.30)
Latvia (para. 34.35)
Netherlands (para. 37.70)
Russian Federation (para. 41.10)
St. Vincent and the Grenadines (para. 41.80)
Slovak Republic (para. 42.65)
Switzerland (para. 43.70)
Togo (para. 44.30)
Venezuela (para. 46.60)

Delete
Czechoslovakia (para. 27.60)

Level II

Add
Bosnia–Herzegovina (para. 23.90)
Croatia (para. 27.35)
Macedonia (para. 35.20)
Montenegro (para. 37.00)
San Marino (but note, remuneration rights only, see para. 42.00)
Serbia (para. 42.35)
Slovenia (para. 42.68)

Duration of Protection (Performers' Rights)　　　　　　　　　　7B.22

Delete
Finland (para. 29.20)

Level IV

Add
Jamaica (para. 33.10)

(2) Duration of protection (Performers' rights)

The following amendments result from the new legislation noted in the Synopsis of Laws (para. 21.00 *et seq.*).　　7B.22

E.U. Member States

E.U. Member States will be required, as from July 1, 1995, to have legislation granting a basic term of 50 years' protection in respect of performances, in accordance with E.C. Directive 93/98 (see paras. 7.51C, 20.20). The countries which will have to institute the requisite 50 year term of protection for performers (or increase their present terms to that level) are Belgium, Ireland, Italy, Luxembourg and Spain. Accordingly, these countries should be added to the list of countries granting performers 50 years' protection or more when the relevant legislation is in place. Furthermore, upon implementation of the new legislation, it will be necessary to delete Ireland, Italy, Luxembourg and Spain from the listing of countries granting performers protection for less than 50 years.

Countries granting performers 50 years' protection or more

Add
Bolivia (para. 23.80)
Bulgaria (para. 24.70)
Chile (para. 25.90)
Czech Republic (para. 27.70)
El Salvador (para. 28.50)
Estonia (para. 28.60)
Finland (para. 29.20)
Iceland (para. 32.10)

Japan (para. 33.20)
Latvia (para. 34.35)
Netherlands (para. 37.70)
Russian Federation (para. 41.10)
Slovak Republic (para. 42.65)
Switzerland (para. 43.70)
Venezuela (para. 46.60)

Delete
Czechoslovakia (para. 27.60)

Countries granting performers protection, but for less than 50 years

Add
Bosnia-Herzegovina (para. 23.90)
Croatia (para. 27.35)
Jordan (para. 33.30)
Macedonia (para. 35.20)
Montenegro (para. 37.00)
St. Vincent and the Grenadines (para. 41.80)
Serbia (para. 42.35)
Slovenia (para. 42.68)
Togo (para. 44.30)

Delete
Chile (para. 25.90)
El Salvador (para. 28.50)
Finland (para. 29.20)
Iceland (para. 32.10)
Japan (para. 33.20)

Countries not specifying period of protection

San Marino (para. 42.00)

(3) Private copying and rental (Performers' rights)

Performers' participation in private copying payments

7B.23   In the following additional countries, performers participate in private copying payments: Czech Republic, Denmark, Estonia, Greece, Italy,

PRIVATE COPYING AND RENTAL (PERFORMERS' RIGHTS)   7B.24

Japan, the Netherlands, Russian Federation, Slovak Republic, United States of America. See paragraph 20.28.

Performers' specific rental rights

In the following additional countries (and apart from E.U. countries), performers have been granted specific rights concerning rental: Austria, Bulgaria, Czech Republic, Latvia, Russian Federation, Slovak Republic. See paragraph 20.31.

By virtue of E.C. Directive 92/100, performers have a specific rental right in all European Union Member States: see paragraphs 7.51A, 20.20.

(4) Non-protecting countries (Performers' rights)   7B.24

Countries not granting specific rights to performers

African Region

Delete
Togo (para. 44.30)

Carribean Region

Delete
Jamaica (para. 33.10)
St. Vincent and the Grenadines (para. 41.80)

Central and South America

Delete
Bolivia (para. 23.80)
Venezuela (para. 46.60)

Europe

Delete
Bulgaria (para. 24.70)
Netherlands (para. 37.70)

Note: Belgium is to be deleted when the legislation implementing E.C. Directive 92/100 is adopted: see paragraph 20.20.

Middle East

Delete
Jordan (para. 33.30)

APPENDIX C

REGIONAL PROTECTION OF PERFORMERS' AND PRODUCERS' RIGHTS

Introductory

7C.01 Amendments resulting from the legislative changes noted in the Synopsis of Laws (para. 21.00 *et seq.*) are set out in paragraphs 7C.02–7C.07 below.

African region

7C.02 *Performers*

Add
Togo (para. 44.30)

Phonogram producers

Add
Namibia (para. 37.40)
Togo (para. 44.30)

Video/film/cinematographic work producers

(a) Specific producer's right

Add
Angola (para. 21.60)
Togo (para. 44.30)

[Countries protecting authors of cinematographic works

Add
Togo*]

Asian and Asian Pacific region

Phonogram producers

Taiwan

It should be noted that sound recordings are protected as author's works in Taiwan: there is not a separate producer's right, though the producer may acquire the author's right: see paragraph 44.00.

Carribean region

Performers

Add
Jamaica (para. 33.10)
St. Vincent and the Grenadines (para. 41.80)

Video/film/cinematographic work producers

(a) Specific producer's right

Add
Jamaica (para. 33.10)

7C.05   REGIONAL PROTECTION OF PERFORMERS' AND PRODUCERS' RIGHTS

Delete
St. Vincent and the Grenadines (para. 41.80)

[Countries protecting authors of cinematographic works

Add
St. Vincent and the Grenadines

Delete
Jamaica]

Central and South America

7C.05   *Performers*

Add
Bolivia (para. 23.80)
Venezuela (para. 46.60)

Phonogram producers

Add
Bolivia (para. 23.80)

Video/film/cinematographic work producers

[Countries protecting authors of cinematographic works

Correction. Venezuela: add asterisk]

Europe

7C.06   In consulting the listings in main text paragraph 7C.06, note, in connection with the United Kingdom, the special position of the Isle of Man: see paragraph 32.70.

Performers

Add
Bosnia-Herzegovina (para. 23.90)
Bulgaria (para. 24.70)
Croatia (para. 27.35)
Czech Republic (para. 27.70)
Estonia (para. 28.60)
Latvia (para. 34.35)
Macedonia (para. 35.20)
Montenegro (para. 37.00)
Netherlands (para. 37.70)
Russian Federation (para. 41.10)
Serbia (para. 42.35)
Slovak Republic (para. 42.65)
Slovenia (para. 42.68)
Switzerland (para. 43.70)

Note: Belgium will be added to the countries protecting performers when the legislation implementing E.C. Directive 92/100 is adopted: see paragraph 20.20.

Delete
Czechoslovakia (para. 27.60)
Union of Soviet Socialist Republics (para. 45.40)

Phonogram producers

Add
Czech Republic (para. 27.70)
Estonia (para. 28.60)
Greece (para. 30.50)
Latvia (para. 34.35)
Netherlands (para. 37.70)
Russian Federation (para. 41.10)
Slovak Republic (para. 42.65)

Note: Belgium will be added to the countries protecting phonogram producers when the legislation implementing E.C. Directive 92/100 is adopted: see paragraph 20.20.

Delete
Czechoslovakia (para. 27.60)
Union of Soviet Socialist Republics (para. 45.40)

Video/film/cinematographic work producers

(a) Specific producer's right

Add
Greece (para. 30.50)
Latvia (para. 34.35)

Note: Belgium, Denmark, Netherlands and Italy will be added when the legislation implementing E.C. Directive 92/100 is adopted: see paragraph 20.20.

Delete
Bulgaria (para. 24.70)
Union of Soviet Socialist Republics (para. 45.40)

(b) Acquired exploitation rights

Add
Armenia (para. 22.00)
Azerbaidjan (para. 22.70)
Belarus (para. 23.25)
Bulgaria (para. 24.70)
Czech Republic (para. 27.70)
Estonia (para. 28.60)
Georgia (para. 30.10)
Kazakhstan (para. 33.60)
Kirghizia (para. 33.75)
Moldova (para. 36.70)
Russian Federation (para. 41.10)
Slovak Republic (para. 42.65)
Tadjikistan (para. 43.90)
Turkmenistan (para. 45.00)
Ukraine (para. 45.35)
Uzbekistan (para. 46.30)

Delete
Czechoslovakia (para. 27.60)

[Countries protecting authors of cinematographic works

Add
Armenia*, Azerbaidjan*, Belarus*, Bosnia-Herzegovina, Croatia, Czech Republic*, Estonia*, Georgia*, Kazakhastan*, Kirghizia*, Macedonia, Moldova*, Montenegro, Russian Federation*, Serbia, Slovak Republic*, Slovenia, Tadjikistan*, Turkmenistan*, Ukraine*, Uzbekistan*.

Note: On the adoption of the legislation implementing E.C. Directive 92/100 it will be necessary to add an asterisk to Belgium, Denmark and Greece, and also to add Ireland*, United Kingdom*: see paragraph 20.20.

Delete
Czechoslovakia*, Union of Soviet Socialist Republics*]

Middle East

Performers 7C.07

Add
Jordan (para. 33.30)

[Countries protecting authors of cinematographic works

Add
Jordan (para. 33.30)]

CHAPTER 8

COMPREHENSIVE PROTECTION

III Adequate standard of protection

For a general survey of the present international situation regarding protection of sound recordings, and the arguments concerning inclusion of 8.04

the sound recording in the Berne Convention, see Agnew, D.E., "Reform in the international protection of sound recordings: upsetting the delicate balance between authors, performers, and producers, or pragmatism in the age of digital piracy" [1992] *Ent. L.R.* 125.

Energetic forms of reproduction and communication

8.15 For a report on the issues discussed at the WIPO Symposium on the impact of digital technology on copyright and neighbouring rights, Harvard 1993, see McDonald, B.W. in *Copyright World* 1993, June, 20.

Acts of reproduction and communication requiring authorisation

8.16 *Pay TV*

For the problems arising in respect of Pay TV, in the context of Australia and the Asia/Pacific region, see Curtis, N., "Satellite-delivered Pay TV services: the copyright issues relating to film" [1992] *Ent. L.R.* 71; Mallam, P., "Legal aspects of the globalisation of Pay TV" [1993] *Ent. L.R.* 43.

Television via telephone

On the United States position and the technical possibilities, see Goodenough, O.R., "Television via telephone lines: regulation and the fibre optic revolution in the United States" [1992] *Ent. L.R.* 66.

PART II

REFERENCE MATERIALS

SYNOPSIS OF LAWS, CHARTS, ETC.

TABLE A: CONVENTION MEMBERSHIP (ADDENDUM)

In addition to those listed in the main text, the following countries have (by accession, ratification or succession) become members of the Conventions as indicated. Further details are given in the Synopsis of Laws. The relevant paragraph numbers are shown in brackets after the countries listed below.

Country	Convention	Reference
Albania* (21.20)	Berne (P94)	*Copyright* 1994, 22
Argentina* (21.90)	Rome	*Copyright* 1992, 29
Australia* (22.30)	Rome rX	*Copyright* 1992, 301
Bolivia* (23.80)	(1) Berne (P93) (2) Rome	*Copyright* 1993, 178 *Copyright* 1994, 22
Bosnia–Herzegovina* (23.90)	(1) Berne (P92) (2) U.C.C. (P74)	*Copyright* 1994, 21 *Copyright* 1994, 16
China* (26.00)	(1) Berne (P92) (2) U.C.C. (GP92) (3) Phonograms	*Copyright* 1992, 145 *Copyright* 1994, 16 *Copyright* 1993, 49
Croatia* (27.35)	(1) Berne (P91) (2) U.C.C. (P74)	*Copyright* 1992, 181 *Copyright* 1994, 16
Cyprus* (27.50)	Phonograms	*Copyright* 1993, 120
Czech Republic* (27.70)	(1) Berne (P93) (2) U.C.C. (P80) (3) Rome r (4) Phonograms	*Copyright* 1993, 17 *Copyright* 1994, 16 *Copyright* 1994, 23 *Copyright* 1994, 23
El Salvador* (28.50)	Berne (P94)	*Copyright* 1993, 271

Country	Convention	Reference
Gambia* (30.00)	Berne (P93)	*Copyright* 1993, 18
Greece* (30.50)	(1) Rome (2) Phonograms	*Copyright* 1993, 19 *Copyright* 1993, 271
Jamaica* (33.10)	(1) Berne (P94) (2) Rome (3) Phonograms	*Copyright* 1993, 243 *Copyright* 1994, 23 *Copyright* 1993, 254
Kazakhstan* (33.60)	U.C.C. (G73)	*Copyright* 1994, 16
Kenya* (33.70)	Berne (P93)	*Copyright* 1993, 61
Macedonia* (35.20)	Berne (P93)	*Copyright* 1993, 177
Namibia* (37.40)	Berne (P93)	*Copyright* 1993, 243
Netherlands* (37.70)	(1) Rome r (2) Phonograms	*Copyright* 1993, 253 *Copyright* 1993, 120
Nigeria (38.50)	(1) Berne (P93) (2) Rome r	*Copyright* 1993, 119 *Copyright* 1993, 253
Russian Federation* (41.10)	U.C.C. (G73)	*Copyright* 1994, 16
St. Lucia* (41.60)	Berne (P93)	*Copyright* 1993, 83
Slovak Republic* (42.65)	(1) Berne (P93) (2) U.C.C. (P80) (3) Rome r (4) Phonograms	*Copyright* 1993, 18 *Copyright* 1994, 16 *Copyright* 1994, 11 *Copyright* 1993, 120
Slovenia* (42.68)	(1) Berne (P92) (2) U.C.C. (P74)	*Copyright* 1992, 145 *Copyright* 1994, 16
Switzerland* (43.70)	(1) Berne (P93) (2) U.C.C. (P93) (3) Rome r (4) Phonograms	*Copyright* 1993, 119 *Copyright* 1994, 16 *Copyright* 1993, 254 *Copyright* 1993, 120

SYNOPSIS OF LAWS, CHARTS, ETC.   20.11

Country	Convention	Reference
Tadjikistan (43.90)	U.C.C. (G73)	*Copyright* 1994, 16
Uruguay* (46.20)	U.C.C. (GP93)	*Copyright* 1994, 16

© J.A.L. Sterling 1994

Notes
(1) An asterisk in the above list indicates membership of the WIPO Convention. In addition to those indicated in this list and the main text (Table A: Addendum note), the following countries have, since October 1991, become members of the WIPO Convention, by accession or succession: Armenia, Bhutan, Estonia, Latvia, Lithuania, Moldova, Uzbekistan.
[Post January 1, 1994: Brunei Darussalam, Georgia.]
(2) The reference for Spain, Rome 1991 r, in the main text Addendum, is *Copyright* 1991, 221.
(3) For new memberships of the Audiovisual Works Registration Treaty, see paragraph 7.49; and of the Satellites Convention, see paragraph 20.12.
(4) In Table A, the entry for Czechoslovakia is replaced by the entries for the Czech Republic and the Slovak Republic; the entry for the U.S.S.R. is replaced by the entries for the successor States, and the entry for Yugoslavia is modified by the entries for the Successor States (see para. 21.00).

[January 1994]

APPENDIX TO TABLE A

(d) *Satellites Convention* 1974

Armenia has acceded to the Satellites Convention, with effect from December 13, 1993: see *Copyright* 1994, 23.

Australia should be included in the main text list of members of the Convention, having become a party on October 26, 1990 (*correction*).

Croatia has succeeded to the membership of Yugoslavia: see *Copyright* 1993, 255.

Greece became a party to the Convention on October 27, 1991: see *Copyright* 1992, 10.

The Russian Federation continues the U.S.S.R. membership: see *Copyright* 1992, 28.

Slovenia became a party to the Convention on June 25, 1991: see *Copyright* 1994, 13.

Switzerland has ratified the Convention, with effect from September 24, 1993: see *Copyright* 1993, 254.

[January 1994]

SUMMARY OF NATIONAL LAW PROVISIONS

Amendments

20.20 Amendments to Lists I to V (main text paras. 20.22–20.34) and to the Summary Chart (main text para. 20.51) resulting from the new legislation noted in the Synopsis of Laws (para. 21.00 *et seq.*) are set out in the corresponding paragraphs below.

E.U. Member States

The particular situation as regards the amendments resulting from implementation of E.C. Directives 92/100 (rental and lending rights, and related rights) and 93/98 (term of protection) (see paras. 7.51A, 7.51C) are noted in the paragraphs relating to each respective List and the Summary Chart.

The present members of the European Union are Belgium, Denmark, France, Germany, Greece, Ireland, Italy, Luxembourg, the Netherlands, Portugal, Spain and the United Kingdom. Austria, Finland, Norway and Sweden are in the process of joining the European Union.

When the changes resulting from E.C. Directives 92/100 and 93/98 have been effected, all European Union Member States will grant protection on the lines of the following format.

Literary, dramatic, musical and artistic works: Level I(m) protection for authors (70 years p.m.a.).

Performances: Level I, Ix, II or IIx protection for performers (50 years).

Sound recordings: Level I, Ix, II or IIx protection for producers (50 years).

Cinematographic works: Level I(m) protection for author(s) (who must include director) (70 years after the death of the last survivor of the specified categories of author).

Film fixations: Level IV (or higher) protection for producers (50 years).

Broadcasts: Protection in accordance with E.C. Directive 92/100.

Rental and lending rights will have been or will be accorded to authors, performers and phonogram and film fixation producers (see para. 20.31).

LIST 1: LEVELS OF PROTECTION

Cabling

With reference to the inclusion of cabling within the ambit of Article 12 of the Rome Convention, see Dreier, T., *Kabelweiterleitung und Urheberrecht—eine vergleichende Darstellung* (Beck'sche, 1991).

20.22 *Phonographic recordings/works*

Belgium and Luxembourg will be added to Level I or II when the legislation implementing E.C. Directive 92/100 is adopted: see paragraph 20.20.

Cinematographic recordings/works"

On the implementation of E.C. Directive 92/100 it is necessary for each European Union Member State to introduce protection for film fixation producers at Level IV (or higher). France, Germany, Portugal, Spain and (by the 1993 legislation) Greece, already grant protection both to authors of cinematographic works and, separately, to film fixation producers. It should be noted that entries for Belgium, Denmark, Ireland, Italy, Luxembourg, the Netherlands and the United Kingdom will need to be inserted at the appropriate levels when the legislation implementing E.C. Directive 92/100 is adopted: see paragraph 20.20.

LEVEL I

Phonographic recordings/works

Add:
Bolivia (para. 23.80)
Chile (para. 25.90)
China (para. 26.00)
Czech Republic (para. 27.70)
Estonia (para. 28.60)
Finland (para. 29.20)
Greece (para. 30.50)
Jamaica (para. 33.10)
Netherlands (para. 37.70)
Russian Federation (para. 41.10)
St. Vincent and the Grenadines (para. 41.80)
Slovak Republic (para. 42.65)
Switzerland (para. 43.70)
Togo (para. 44.30)
Venezuela (para. 46.60)

Delete:
Czechoslovakia (para. 27.60)

Cinematographic recordings/works

Add:
Angola (para. 21.60)

Synopsis of Laws, Charts, etc.   20.22

Armenia (para. 22.00)
Azerbaidjan (para. 22.70)
Bahrain (para. 22.95)
Belarus (para. 23.45)
Bosnia-Herzegovina (para. 23.90)
China: **add** asterisk; **delete** (cw) (para. 26.00)
Croatia (para. 27.35)
Czech Republic (para. 27.70)
Estonia (para. 28.60)
Georgia (para. 30.10)
Jamaica (para. 33.10)
Jordan (para. 33.30)
Kazakhstan (para. 33.60)
Kirghizia (para. 33.75)
Latvia (para. 34.35)
Lithuania (para. 34.90)
Macedonia (para. 35.20)
Moldova (para. 36.70)
Montenegro (para. 37.00)
Namibia (para. 37.40)
Russian Federation (para. 41.10)
Serbia (para. 42.35)
Slovak Republic (para. 42.65)
Slovenia (para. 42.68)
Tadjikistan (para. 43.90)
Turkmenistan (para. 45.00)
Ukraine (para. 45.35)
United Arab Emirates (para. 45.60)
Uzbekistan (para. 46.30)

Note: **add** asterisk to Greece (para. 30.50).

Delete
Czechoslovakia (para. 27.60)

LEVEL II

Phonographic recordings/works

Add:
Latvia (para. 34.35)

Delete
China (para. 26.00)

Finland (para. 29.20)
Jamaica (para. 33.10)
St. Vincent and the Grenadines (para. 41.80)

Cinematographic recordings/works

Delete
China (v) (para. 26.00)
(Jamaica) (para. 33.10)

LEVEL IV

Phonographic recordings/works

Add:
Mexico (para. 36.50)
Namibia (para. 37.40)

Delete
Chile (para. 25.90)
Switzerland (para. 43.70)
Venezuela (para. 46.60)

Note: References to the United Kingdom cover the Isle of Man (see para. 32.70.)

Notes

Two objects of protection

20.23   *Correction.* **Delete** "at Level I" in the first line of the main text.

LIST II: DURATION OF PROTECTION

SECTION A: COUNTRIES GRANTING 50 YEARS' PROTECTION OR MORE

Phonographic recordings/works

Add:
20.25   Bolivia (para. 23.80)

Synopsis of Laws, Charts, etc.   20.25

Bulgaria (para. 24.70)
Chile (para. 25.90)
Cyprus (para. 27.50)
Czech Republic (para. 27.70)
El Salvador (para. 28.50)
Estonia (para. 28.60)
Finland (para. 29.20)
Greece (para. 30.50)
Iceland (para. 32.10)
Latvia (para. 34.35)
Namibia (para. 37.40)
Netherlands (para. 37.70)
Norway: see main text paragraph 38.90 (*Correction*)
Russian Federation (para. 41.10)
San Marino (para. 42.00)
Slovak Republic (para. 42.65)
Switzerland (para. 43.70)
Taiwan (para. 44.00)
Venezuela (para. 46.60)

Note: Belgium, Germany, Italy, Luxembourg and Spain will be added when the legislation implementing E.C. Directive 92/100 is adopted (see para. 20.20). Accordingly, Germany, Italy, Luxembourg and Spain will then be deleted from Section B (countries granting less than 50 years' protection).

Delete:
Czechoslovakia (para. 27.60)
St. Vincent and the Grenadines (para. 41.80)

Cinematographic recordings/works

Add:
Angola (para. 21.60)
Bahrain (para. 22.95)
Bosnia-Herzegovina (para. 23.90)
Croatia (para. 27.35)
Czech Republic (para. 27.70)
El Salvador (para. 28.50)
Estonia (para. 28.60)
Latvia (para. 34.35)
Macedonia (para. 35.20)
Montenegro (para. 37.00)
Namibia (para. 37.40)
Russian Federation (para. 41.10)
Serbia (para. 42.35)

Slovak Republic (para. 42.65)
Slovenia (para. 42.68)
Taiwan (para. 44.00)

Note: Delete brackets around Jamaica (para. 33.10).

Note: On the implementation of E.C. Directive 92/100, all European Union States will grant (in so far as they do not do so already) protection both to the author(s) of cinematographic works (basic term 70 years p.m.a.) and to the producers of film fixations (term 50 years). Accordingly, the letter (w) after Germany and Spain in Section A will be deleted, there will be an indication that each European Union State grants 50 years' protection or more in respect of both cinematographic works and film fixations, and Germany and Spain will be deleted from Section B.

Delete:
Czechoslovakia (para. 27.60)

SECTION B: COUNTRIES GRANTING LESS THAN 50 YEARS' PROTECTION

Phonographic recordings/works

Add:
St. Vincent and the Grenadines (para. 41.80)
Togo (para. 44.30)

Delete:
Bulgaria (para. 24.70)
Chile (para. 25.90)
Cyprus (para. 27.50)
El Salvador (para. 28.50)
Finland (para. 29.20)
Iceland (para. 32.10)
Norway: see main text paragraph 38.90 (*Correction*)
San Marino (para. 42.00)
Taiwan (para. 44.00)
Venezuela (para. 46.60)

Cinematographic recordings/works

Add
Armenia (para. 22.00)

Azerbaidjan (para. 22.70)
Belarus (para. 23.45)
Georgia (para. 30.10)
Jordan (para. 33.30)
Kazakhstan (para. 33.60)
Kirghizia (para. 33.75)
Lithuania (para. 34.90)
Moldova (para. 36.70)
Tadjikistan (para. 43.90)
Turkmenistan (para. 45.00)
Ukraine (para. 45.35)
United Arab Emirates (para. 45.60)
Uzbekistan (para. 46.30)

Delete:
El Salvador (para. 28.50)
Taiwan (para. 44.00)

Note: References to the United Kingdom cover the Isle of Man: see paragraph 32.70.

Notes

Delete the reference to Jordan: see paragraph 33.30.   20.26

LIST III: RECORDING MACHINE AND TAPE PAYMENTS: NATIONAL LAWS

(See fold-out list on p. 479 in the main text)

European Union

The European Commission is carrying out studies in connection with the possible   20.28
harmonisation of European Union laws in respect of remuneration for private copying (see para. 7.51D).

The majority of European Union States now have laws establishing a system of payment of authors, performers and producers in respect of private copying, namely: Denmark, France, Germany, Greece, Italy, the Netherlands, Portugal and Spain. Consequently, only Belgium, Ireland, Luxembourg and the United Kingdom are without such a system at present.

Private copying remuneration systems are also established in the majority of the EFTA countries: Austria, Finland, Iceland and Switzerland. Norway and Sweden have tax provisions (see main text para. 20.29), so Liechtenstein would appear to be the only EFTA country which has no legislation in the area at present.

Australia

The High Court of Australia has declared unconstitutional the legislation introducing the blank tape payment: see paragraph 22.30.

Bulgaria

New provisions concerning blank tape payments were instituted by the Author's Right and Neighbouring Rights Law 1993 (art. 26). However, the same general structure remains, so that the List III column entries in the main text, apart from those under "Law" and "Effective Date", are still applicable.

Article 26(2) of the 1993 Law provides that 20 per cent. of the sums collected shall be paid to the responsible Ministry for cultural purposes.

See paragraph 24.70.

Czechoslovakia

The entry in List III should be deleted, with substitution of entries for the Czech Republic and the Slovak Republic: see paragraphs 27.70, 42.65.

Czech Republic

Apart from "Law" and "Effective date", the List III entry is the same as existing entry for Czechoslovakia: see paragraph 27.70.

Denmark

By the amending Law No. 338 of May 14, 1992, a system of payment on blank audio and video tapes has been introduced in Denmark.

The Law covers tapes, etc., suitable for the making of copies for private use, where the works concerned have been broadcast, released on phonograms or videograms, etc.

The fee is payable by the manufacturer or importer of audio or video tapes, and the distributable sums are shared by authors, performers and producers, less one third, which is applied for cultural purposes.

For 1993, the fee payable for one minute of playing time was 0.045 Dkr. for audio tapes and 0.0625 Dkr. for video tapes (adjustable annually). See Banke L.M. and Shønning P., "New remuneration schemes in Denmark" *Copyright World* 1993, March, 33.

See Neumann, P. and Ehlers, M.R., "Denmark's new levy on blank audio and video tapes to compensate authors and creative artists for private copying" [1993] *Ent. L.R. 25.*

Estonia

Under article 27 of the Law on Author's Right and Neighbouring Rights 1992 (see para. 28.60) a system of recording equipment and blank tape payments is introduced in respect of recording of audiovisual works and sound recordings for private purposes. The payment is to be made by manufacturers and importers of audio and video recording equipment and blank tapes. The participants are the authors, performers and phonogram producers involved. The rate is fixed annually by the Ministry of Culture.

There are exemptions in respect of equipment and tapes which are exported, used for professional recording, and for persons with impaired eyesight or hearing, or otherwise exempted by law.

France

The provisions of articles 31 to 37 of the 1985 Law are incorporated in article L. 311 of the Code of Intellectual Property 1992: see paragraph 29.30.

The remuneration is administered through designated bodies (art. L.311–6). The remuneration for private copying of phonograms is shared as follows: 50 per cent. for authors, 25 per cent. for performers, and 25 per cent. for phonogram producers (art. L.311–7). The remuneration for private copying of videograms is shared equally among the authors, the performers and the videogram producers.

Greece

Under article 18(1) of the Law of March 3, 1993, legally published works may be reproduced for private use.

Under article 18(3), a reasonable remuneration is to be paid to the author of the work and the owners of the neighbouring rights where the reproduction takes place by use of:

 (a) audio or visual or audiovisual recording devices;
 (b) audio or video tapes and other audio or visual or audiovisual recording material;

(c) photocopying machines;
(d) special photocopying paper;
(e) computers.

The remuneration is fixed at:
(a) 6 per cent. of the value of the recording devices, and of the recording material;
(b) 4 per cent. of the value of the photocopying machines, and of the photocopying paper;
(c) 2 per cent. of the value of the computers.

The payment is made by the manufacturers, importers or dealers, and is collected by the respective administration society.

The payments are distributed as follows:

(a) Payments regarding audio and audio/video recording devices, and audio and audio/video tapes: authors 55 per cent., performers 25 per cent., producers 20 per cent.
(b) Payments regarding photocopying machines, special photocopying paper and computers: 50/50 authors and publishers of works.

Tariffs and distribution rules are fixed by Presidential Decree, following a proposal by the Minister of Culture.

By comparison with other laws in the field, the Greek system is notable for its application to special photocopying paper and computers.

Italy

Under the Law of February 5, 1992, No. 93, a right is granted to (a) authors, (b) producers of phonograms, (c) original producers of audiovisual works, and (d) producers of videograms, and their successors in title, to obtain, as compensation for the private reproduction for personal non-commercial use of phonograms and videograms, a payment based on the wholesale price of audio and video recording tapes and similar recording supports, and on audio recording machines. The payments are fixed at:

(a) 10 per cent. of the wholesale price for audio tapes and similar recording supports.;
(b) 5 per cent. of the wholesale price for video tapes and similar recording supports;
(c) 3 per cent. of the wholesale price for audio recording machines.

The payment is to be made by the manufacturer or importer.

The administration is to be undertaken by the Italian Society of Authors and Publishers (SIAE), and the sharing is:

(a) of payments in respect of audio tapes and similar recording supports, and machines: 50 per cent. authors, 50 per cent. producers of phonograms (who must pay 50 per cent. of their share to the relevant performers);
(b) of payments in respect of video tapes and similar recording supports: 33⅓ per cent. authors, 33⅓ per cent. original producers of audiovisual works, 33⅓ per cent. to videogram producers, less in each case 5 per cent. to be paid to IMAIE (Performers Mutual Institute) for professional development of performers.

See Rossbach, C. in *GRUR Int.* 1993, 537 (text of Law, 543).

Japan

By Law No. 106 of December 16, 1992 (text translation in *Copyright* 1993, October) a system of payment of compensation in respect of digital medium recording for private use is instituted. The relevant machines and recording media are specified by Cabinet Order (art. 30(2)). The payment is made on first purchase of the equipment or medium, and the administration of the sums collected is through a designated organisation (arts. 104*bis*—104*quater*). The participants are the authors, performers and phonogram producers concerned (arts. 30(2) and 102). The rates of compensation must be approved by the Commissioner of the Agency for the Cultural Affairs (art. 104*sexies*). Up to 20 per cent. of the compensation is to be used for such activities as the protection of author's rights and neighbouring rights, and the promotion of the creation and dissemination of works (art. 104*octies*).

See Sato, T. and Ohno, S., "Entertainment aspects of Japan's new Copyright Law" [1993] *Ent. L.R.* 89.

The Netherlands

Law 305 of May 30, 1990 instituted the right of authors to obtain remuneration in respect of private copying. A translation of Law 305/1990 appears in *Copyright* 1991, October (reference for entry in last column of List III in the main text). The 1990 Law effects the introduction by inserting arts. 16(c)-(g) in the Author's Right Law 1912. Article 10 of the Law of March 18, 1993, provides that articles 16(c)-(g) of the 1912 Law are to apply in respect of the rights granted to performers, phonogram producers and broadcasting organisations.

Thus the words "Performers, Producers, Broadcasting Organisations" should be added after "Authors" in the Participants column of List III.

Nigeria

Section 32C inserted in the Copyright Decree 1988 by the Copyright (Amendment) Decree 1992 provides that a levy shall be paid on any material used or capable of being used to infringe copyright in a work. The amount of the levy is determined by the Minister, and paid into a Fund for disbursement amongst approved societies. The beneficiaries are not at present specified. The publication of the relevant orders and regulations is awaited.

Russian Federation

Article 26 of the Law of July 9, 1993 establishes a system of remuneration for authors, performers and phonogram producers, in respect of the private copying of audiovisual works and phonograms.

The remuneration is paid by the manufacturers or importers of audio and video recording equipment, and of audio and video recording material (tapes, blank CDs, etc.) (art. 26(2)).

The remuneration is administered collectively, and, except as otherwise agreed, is to be shared as follows: authors 40 per cent., performers 30 per cent., phonogram producers 30 per cent. (art. 26(2)).

The amount of remuneration is determined by agreement, or, failing agreement, by an agency of the Russian Federation specially empowered in this respect (art. 26(2)).

There are exceptions for exported equipment and material, and professional equipment (art. 26(3)).

Slovak Republic

Apart from "Law" and "Effective date", the List III entry in the main text is the same as the existing entry for Czechoslovakia: see paragraph 42.65.

Spain

Law 20/1992 of July 7, 1992 rewords the provisions of article 25 of Law 22/1987, retaining the general system of remuneration, and specifying the amounts to be paid by manufacturers or importers, as follows (art. 25(4)):

(a) (Provisions concerning payments on equipment for reproduction of books).
(b) Equipment for reproduction of phonograms: 100 Ptas. per unit of recording.
(c) Equipment for reproduction of videograms: 1,100 Ptas. per unit of recording.
(d) Sound recording material: 30 Ptas. per hour of recording.
(e) Visual or audiovisual recording material: 50 Ptas. per hour of recording.

Article 25(5)-(10) as amended contains provisions as to payment procedures.

For other regulations concerning the application of article 25, see Decree 1434/92 of November 27, 1992.

Switzerland

Article 20(3) of the Law of October 9, 1992 provides that manufacturers and importers of audio and video recording material must pay the author a remuneration in respect of the use of works for private purposes, as provided by article 19.

The remuneration can only be claimed through an approved administration society (art. 20(4)).

United States of America

The Audio Home Recording Act 1992 added sections 1001–1010 to the U.S. Copyright Act 1976. These sections establish a new Chapter concerning the importation and distribution of digital audio recording devices (*i.e.* digital recording machines) and digital recording media (*i.e.* tapes or discs for use in the recording devices). Non-commercial copying of digital and analogue recordings is not subject to action for infringement, and manufacturers and distributors cannot be sued for contributory infringement in this connection (s.1008).

On the other hand, a system of royalty payments is instituted, similar in principle to those adopted in other countries to afford compensation to rightowners for private copying.

The royalty rates are fixed in section 1004 at:

— 2 per cent. of the transfer price of the digital audio recording device, to be paid by the importer or distributor (minimum $1, maximum $8 per single machine; $12 per multiple recording machine)
— 3 per cent. of the transfer price of digital media, to be paid by the importer or distributor.

The royalties are to be paid to the Copyright Office, $66\frac{2}{3}$ per cent. going to the Sound Recording Fund, $33\frac{1}{3}$ per cent. to the Musical Works Fund.
The payments to the Sound Recording Fund are to be divided as follows (s.1006(b)(1)):

— 4 per cent. to non-featured performers;
— 96 per cent. to be divided 60/40 between owners of rights in sound recordings, and featured performers.

The payments to the Musical Works Fund are to be divided 50/50 between music publishers and composers/songwriters (s.1006(b)(2)).

The entitlement to participation is related to distribution of the sound recording in the United States.

The United States Copyright Office is in the process of formulating the regulations for the implementation of the 1992 Act: see 40 *J. Copr. Soc'y* 506–507 (1993); 41 *J. Copr. Soc'y* 126 (1993).

See Berman, J., "The Audio Home Recording Act of 1991: a road to compromise" [1992] *Ent. L.R.* 64, and Thall, P. in [1993] *Ent. L.R.* E–49.

Bibliography

For an extensive survey of private copying laws, with details of remuneration rates and distribution systems, see Davies G. and Hung M., *Music and Video Private Copying* (Sweet & Maxwell, 1993).

Notes

Bulgaria

20.29   See the note under paragraph 20.28.

LIST IV: RENTAL RIGHTS: NATIONAL LAWS

E.C. Directive 92/100

20.31   By reason of E.C. Directive 92/100, rental and lending rights must (in so far as they do not already exist) be introduced for the benefit of authors, performers, phonogram producers and film fixation producers in all European Union Member States by July 1, 1994: see paragraph 7.51A.

Consequently, when the requisite legislation is in place, the names of the following countries will figure in each of the four columns of List IV: Belgium, Denmark, France, Germany, Greece, Ireland, Italy, Luxembourg, the Netherlands, Portugal, Spain and the United Kingdom.

Austria

Under the provisions of the amending Law UrhRG Nov. 1993 (see *GRUR Int.* 1993, 792), a new article (16a) is inserted in the 1936 Law, specifically providing for rental (commercial) and lending (non-commercial) rights for authors, performers, producers of phonographic records, moving image picture producers and broadcasters.

The right is exclusive in respect of rental, and is for equitable remuneration in respect of lending (1936 Law, as amended, art. 16a(1)-(3)). The rental and lending rights of the various rightowners are specified by the combined effect of articles 16(3), 16a, 67(2), 74(7), 76(6) and 76a(5) of the 1936 Law as amended by the 1993 Law: these amendments come into effect on January 1, 1994. There are some special provisions regarding the author's right to a share of the rental and lending remuneration received by the licence of film producers (art. 16a(5)).

Add: "Austria" to all four columns of List IV.

Bolivia

Under the Law of April 13, 1992, phonogram producers are granted the rental right.

Add: "Bolivia" to the second column of List IV.

Bulgaria

Under the Law of June 16, 1993, the author is granted the right to authorise distribution of copies of his work (art. 18(2)(2)); the performer is granted the right to authorise distribution of recordings of his performance (art. 76(1)); the phonogram producer has the right to authorise distribution of his recordings (art. 86(1)(1)). "Distribution" includes rental (see Additional Provisions, arts. 2(4) and 3). The Law of March 30, 1990, to which reference is made in main text paragraph 20.32, has been repealed.

Add: "Bulgaria" to the first three columns of List IV.

Canada

Section 2.1(h) of the Copyright Act, inserted by the 1993 Act, c.44, establishes a rental right in respect of computer programs; section 5(4) as amended by the same Act includes the rental right in the copyright in records.

Add: "Canada" to the second column of List IV.

Chile

Under Law No. 19.166 of September 9, 1992, (art. 1(9)), the phonogram producer is, by amendment of article 68 of Law 17.336/1970, granted the exclusive right to authorise or prohibit rental of his phonograms.

Add: "Chile" to the second column of List IV.

China

Article 9(5) of the Law of September 7, 1990 includes "distribution" among the author's exploitation rights. Renting is included in the definition of "distribution" in article 5 of the Implementing Regulations of May 24, 1991: see *Copyright* 1991, November.

Producers of domestic sound and video recordings may have the rental right. Certain foreign producers of sound and video recordings have the rental right: see paragraph 26.00.

In consequence, "China" may be added to the four columns of List IV.

Cyprus

A rental right for authors and film producers is introduced by the Copyright (Amendment) Act 1993: see paragraph 27.50.

Consequently "Cyprus" should be added to the first, third and fourth columns of List IV.

Czech Republic

Article 13(2) of the Law No. 35 of March 25, 1965, as modified and amended by the Law No. 89 of March 28, 1990, and Federal Law No. 468 of November 1, 1991, introduces for authors, performers, phonogram producers and broadcasting organisations a remuneration right in respect of rental. The right can only be claimed through the organisation accredited by the Ministry of Culture, which also fixes rates and distribution methods (arts. 13(2) and 44).

Add: "Czech Republic" to the first three columns of List IV. See generally, paragraph 27.70.

Denmark

The lending of records, tapes, etc., by municipal libraries has been held to constitute rental falling under the provisions of the 1961 Law and requiring the licence of the rightowner: *Nordisk Copyright Bureau v. Municipality of Søllerød* [1994] EIPR D-6.

El Salvador

Under Decree 604 of July 15, 1993, rights of rental (*arrendamiento*) are granted to authors concerning their works (art. 7(d)) and to phonogram producers (art. 83).

Add: "El Salvador" to the first three columns of List IV.

Estonia

Under the law on Author's Right and Neighbouring Rights 1992 (see para. 28.60), exclusive rental rights are granted to (a) authors (art. 13(2)), and (b) phonogram producers (art. 70(2)).

Add: "Estonia" to the first three columns of List IV.

Finland

By the amending Law No. 34 of January 11, 1991, a rental right is introduced for authors of literary and musical works: see *Copyright* 1992, April.

Add: "Finland" to the first and third columns of List IV.

France

The provisions of articles 1(1) and 31(3) of the 1957 Law, and of articles 21 and 26 of the 1985 Law are incorporated in articles L.111–1, L.131–3, L.213–1 and L.215–1 respectively of the Code of Intellectual Property 1992: see paragraph 29.30.

Greece

The Law of March 3, 1993 provides renting and public lending rights:

    (a) for authors (art. 3(1)(d), with unwaivable right to remuneration (art. 34(4));
    (b) for performers (art. 46(2)(b));
    (c) for sound, or sound/visual recording producers (art. 47(1));
    (d) for broadcasting organisations (art. 48(1)(d)).

Add: "Greece" to all four columns in List IV.

Iceland

See paragraph 32.10: details awaited.

Isle of Man

Section 18(2) of the Copyright Act 1991 establishes the rental right in relation to sound recordings, films and computer programs, through exception to the exhaustion rule applying to the right to issue copies of the work to the public (s. 18(1)). The position is thus the same as under the U.K. Copyright, Designs and Patents Act 1988 (see main text para. 20.32). The beneficiaries of the rental right are the makers of sound recordings and films, and the authors of computer programs.

Add: "Isle of Man" to the second and fourth columns of List IV.

Italy

It is reported that the Turin High Court of Appeal (*Cassazione*) has ruled that the author's right under the Law of April 22, 1941 extends to rental: see *Billboard*, March 5, 1994.

Jamaica

Under the Copyright Act 1993, owners of copyright in sound recordings, films and computer programs enjoy rental rights: see sections 2(1) "rental", 3(2)).

Add: "Jamaica" to the second and fourth columns of List IV.

Latvia

Under the Law of May 11, 1993, authors, performers and sound recording producers are granted exclusive rental rights (arts. 14(2)(2), 40(1)(7) and 43(1)). There are specific provisions concerning the administration of this right (arts. 40(4), 43(4) and 51).

Add: "Latvia" to the first three columns of List IV.

Russian Federation

The Law of July 9, 1993 establishes rental rights for authors (art. 16(2), specifically within the distribution right), performers (art. 37(2)(5)) and phonogram producers (art. 38(2)(3)).

The performer's rental right relates to commercially published phonograms; the right passes to the phonogram producer, the performer retaining the right to remuneration (art. 37(2)(5)).

Add: "Russian Federation" to the first three columns of List IV.

St. Vincent and the Grenadines

Under the Copyright Act 1989, "distribution" means the distribution to the public, for commercial purposes, of copies of a work or production by way of rental, lease, hire, loan or similar means (s.2).

The phonogram producer has the exclusive right of distributing (and hence of renting, etc.) any reproduction of the phonogram, the original sound recording of which was lawfully made in St. Vincent and the Grenadines. Under section 45,

SYNOPSIS OF LAWS, CHARTS, ETC.   20.31

reciprocal treatment may be given where similar rights are granted in another country.

It would seem that rental rights are not specifically granted to authors and performers.

Add: "St. Vincent and the Grenadines" to the second column of List IV.

San Marino

It would appear that authors have rental rights under the Law of January 25, 1991: see paragraph 42.00.

Pending clarification, it is not proposed to enter San Marino in List IV.

Slovak Republic

Add: "Slovak Republic" to the first three columns of List IV. See above, Czech Republic, and paragraph 42.65.

Switzerland

Article 13(1) of the Law of October 9, 1992 grants authors of literary and artistic works a right to remuneration in respect of the rental of copies of such works. The remuneration may only be claimed through an approved collecting society (art. 13(3)). Authors of computer programs, however, have an exclusive rental right (art. 10(3)).

Add: "Switzerland" to the first and third columns of List IV.

Taiwan

Article 29 of the Law of June 10, 1992 provides that the author shall have the exclusive right to rent his/her work to others.

Audiovisual works and sound recordings are works (art. 5(7)(8)), and therefore the authors of these works have the rental right. However, the producer is not defined as an author in this context, or given a separate rental right. Consequently, Taiwan should be entered only in columns one and three of List IV; "Taiwan" in columns two and four is to be deleted.

Nevertheless, it should be noted that in practice the producer may acquire the rental right from the author by contract.

Venezuela

Under article 41 of the Law of August 14, 1993, the owner of the work exploitation right has the right to authorise rental of sold copies. The phonogram producer has a similar right (art. 95). It would seem that the producer of the audiovisual work does not have a rental right separate from that which he acquires by virtue of cession of the author's exploitation rights under article 15.

Add: "Venezuela" to the first three columns of List IV.

NAFTA

Note: It may be anticipated that, by virtue of the provisions of Articles 1705(2)(d) and 1706(1) of the NAFTA Agreement, the rental right for authors and phonogram producers will be introduced (or extended) in Canada, Mexico and the United States: see paragraph 7.55.

Notes

Japan

20.32 The date reference to the 1991 Law is May 2, 1991 (not April 24, 1991). The text translation is reproduced in *Copyright* 1992, January.

LIST V: COUNTRIES WITH NO SPECIFIC PROTECTION IN THE PHONOGRAPHIC OR CINEMATOGRAPHIC CATEGORIES

Bhutan

20.34 Bhutan has acceded to the WIPO Convention: **add** asterisk.

Delete:
Angola* (para. 21.60)
Bahrain (para. 22.95)
Namibia* (n) (para. 37.40)
United Arab Emirates* (n) (para. 45.60)

[*Post* January 1, 1994:

Brunei Darussalam

Brunei Darussalam has acceded to the WIPO Convention (see *Copyright* 1994, 43): **add** asterisk to Brunei.]

SUMMARY CHART

Structure of Chart

The fourth division (Performances). An "x" after the level number indicates that the public performance, broadcasting or cabling rights are for remuneration only (as in the Synopsis, *c.f.* para. 21.00, Levels of protection).

An asterisk in the fourth division indicates a basic protection period of 50 years.

SUMMARY CHART

(See chart on pp. 498–506 in the main text)

Amendments to the Summary Chart resulting from the new legislation noted in the Synopsis of Laws (para. 21.00 *et seq.*) are as follows. Where the amendment is to one element only of the column entry, the whole entry, as amended, is given.

E.C. Directives

Following the implementation of E.C. Directives 92/100 (rental and lending rights, and related rights) and 93/98 (term of protection) (see paras. 7.51A, 7.51C, 20.20), the Summary Chart entries for France and Portugal will remain as in the main text; the additional entry for Greece is shown below (reflecting the 1993 legislation); the entries for Belgium, Denmark, Germany, Ireland, Italy, Luxembourg, the Netherlands, Spain and the United Kingdom will need to be inserted in accordance with the legislation adopted, the net result in all European Union Member States being that phonograms, film fixations and performances will be protected for 50 years, and cinematographic works for 70 years p.m.a. (according to the formula of the Term Directive).

21.60   **ANGOLA** (New entry)
Column (b)(2), **insert** I cw AR* (P)

22.00   **ARMENIA** (New entry)
Column (b)(2), **insert** I cw AR (Pe)

22.70 **AZERBAIDJAN** (New entry)
       Column (b)(2), **insert** I cw AR (Pe)

22.95 **BAHRAIN** (New entry)
       Column (b)(2), **insert** I cw AR* (A)

23.25 **BELARUS** (New entry)
       Column (b)(2), **insert** I cw AR (Pe)

23.80 **BOLIVIA**
       Column (a)(1), **insert** I p NR* (P)
       Performances, **insert** I*

23.90 **BOSNIA-HERZEGOVINA** (New entry)
       Column (b)(2), **insert** I cw AR* (A)
       Performances, **insert** IIx

24.70 **BULGARIA**
       Column (a)(1), **insert** I p NR* (P)
       Column (b)(2), **amend** to I cw AR* (Pe)
       Performances, **insert** I*

25.90 **CHILE**
       Column (a)(1), **amend** to Ix p NR* (P)
       Performances, **amend** to I*

26.00 **CHINA**
       Column (a)(1), **amend** to I sr PR* (P)
       Column (b)(1), **amend** to I v PR* (P)

27.35 **CROATIA** (New entry)
       Column (b)(2), **insert** I cw AR* (A)
       Performances, **insert** IIx

27.50 **CYPRUS**
       Column (a)(1), **amend** to IV sr/w IPR* (P)

27.60 **CZECHOSLOVAKIA**
       Delete entry (see para. 27.60)

27.70 **CZECH REPUBLIC** (New entry)
       Column (a)(1), **insert** I p PR* (P)
       Column (b)(2), **insert** I cw AR* (Pe)
       Performances, **insert** Ix*

Synopsis of Laws, Charts, etc. 20.51

28.50 **EL SALVADOR**
Column (a)(1), **insert** I p PR* (P)
Delete column (a)(2) entries
Column (b)(2) **amend** to I cw AR* (Pe)
Performances, **amend** to Ix*

28.60 **ESTONIA** (New entry)
Column (a)(1), **insert** I p NR* (P)
Column (b)(2), **insert** I aw AR* (Pe)
Performances, **insert** Ix

29.20 **FINLAND**
Column (a)(1), **amend** to Ix sr NR* (P)
Performances, **amend** to Ix*

30.10 **GEORGIA** (New entry)
Column (b)(2), **insert** I cw AR (Pe)

30.50 **GREECE**
Column (a)(1), **insert** Ix p NR* (P)
Column (b)(1), **insert** Ix f NR* (P)
Performances, **amend** to Ix*

32.10 **ICELAND**
Column (a)(1), **amend** to Ix sr NR* (P)
Performances, **amend** to Ix*

32.70 **ISLE OF MAN** (New entry)
Column (a)(1), **insert** I sr C* (P)
Column (b)(1), **insert** I f C* (P)

33.10 **JAMAICA**
Column (a)(1), **insert** I sr C* (P)
Column (b)(1), **insert** I f C* (P)
Performances, **insert** IV

33.20 **JAPAN**
Performances, **amend** to IIx*

33.30 **JORDAN**
Column (b)(2), **insert** I cw AR
Performances, **insert** I

33.60 **KAZAKHSTAN** (New entry)
Column (b)(2), **insert** I cw AR (Pe)

33.75   **KIRGHIZIA** (New entry)
        Column (b)(2), **insert** I cw AR (P)

34.35   **LATVIA** (New entry)
        Column (a)(1), **insert** IIx sr PR* (P)
        Column (b)(2), **insert** I aw AR* (A)
        Performances, **insert** I*

34.90   **LITHUANIA** (New entry)
        Column (b)(2), **insert** I cw AR (Pe)

35.20   **MACEDONIA** (New entry)
        Column (b)(2), **insert** I cw AR* (A)
        Performances, **insert** IIx

36.70   **MOLDOVA** (New entry)
        Column (b)(2), **insert** I cw AR (Pe)

37.00   **MONTENEGRO** (New entry)
        Column (b)(2), **insert** I cw AR* (A)
        Performances, **insert** IIx

37.40   **NAMIBIA** (New entry)
        Column (a)(1), **insert** IV sr C* (P)
        Column (b)(1), **insert** I cf C* (P)

37.70   **NETHERLANDS**
        Column (a)(1), **insert** Ix p NR* (P)
        Performances, **insert** Ix*

38.90   **NORWAY**
        Column (b)(2), **amend** to I cw AR* (A)

41.10   **RUSSIAN FEDERATION** (New entry)
        Column (a)(1), **insert** Ix p NR* (P)
        Column (b)(2), **insert** I aw AR* (Pe)
        Performances, **insert** Ix*

41.80   **ST. VINCENT AND THE GRENADINES**
        Column (a)(1), **amend** to Ix p C(P)
        Delete Column (b)(1) entries
        Column (b)(2), **insert** I aw C* (A)
        Performances, **insert** Ix

SYNOPSIS OF LAWS, CHARTS, ETC. 20.51

42.00 **SAN MARINO**
Delete Column (a)(1) entries
Column (a)(2), **insert** I sr AR* (A)
Performances, **amend** to IIx

42.35 **SERBIA** (New entry)
Column (b)(2), **insert** I cw AR* (A)
Performances, **insert** IIx

42.65 **SLOVAK REPUBLIC** (New entry)
Column (a)(1), **insert** I p PR* (P)
Column (b)(2), **insert** I cw AR* (Pe)
Performances, **insert** Ix*

42.68 **SLOVENIA** (New entry)
Column (b)(2), **insert** I cw AR* (A)
Performances, **insert** IIx

43.70 **SWITZERLAND**
Column (a)(1), **amend** to Ix sr PR* (P)
Performances, **amend** to Ix*

43.60 **SWEDEN**
Column (b)(2), **amend** to I fw AR* (A)

43.90 **TADJIKISTAN** (New entry)
Column (b)(2), **insert** I cw AR

44.00 **TAIWAN**
Column (a)(2), **amend** to I sr AR* (A)
Column (b)(2), **amend** to II aw AR* (A)

44.30 **TOGO**
Column (a)(1), **insert** Ix p PR (P)
Column (b)(2), **amend** to I cw AR* (A)
Performances, **insert** Ix

45.00 **TURKMENISTAN** (New entry)
Column (b)(2), **insert** I cw AR

45.35 **UKRAINE** (New entry)
Column (b)(2), **insert** I cw AR

45.60 **UNITED ARAB EMIRATES** (New entry)
Column (b)(2), **insert** I cw AR (Pe)

79

46.30 UZBEKISTAN (New entry)
Column (b)(2), **insert** I cw AR

46.60 VENEZUELA
Column (a)(1), **amend** to Ix p PR (P)
Performances, **insert** Ix

SYNOPSIS OF LAWS

Introduction

Structure of the entries

21.00 The letter *"m"* after a Level number indicates that moral rights (or rights of a "moral" type) are granted. The precise extent of such rights must be ascertained from the text of the respective law.

Legislative and other developments

Republics which formed part of the U.S.S.R. on May 31, 1991

21.01 Estonia, Latvia and the Russian Federation have adopted new laws on author's right and neighbouring rights (see paras. 28.60, 34.35, 41.10 respectively).

With regard to Lithuania and the other Republics which were formerly part of the U.S.S.R. (Armenia, Azerbaidjan, Belarus, Georgia, Kazakhstan, Kirghizia, Moldova, Tadjikistan, Turkmenistan, Ukraine and Uzbekistan) it is assumed, pending notice of new legislation, that protection continues as it was understood to be under the law applying before May 31, 1991 (see main text para. 45.40), and accordingly all these Republics are separately entered in the Synopsis of Laws under their respective paragraph numbers, the relevant entries also being made in List I (levels: para. 20.22), List II (duration: para. 20.25), the Chart (para. 20.51) and the Index of Countries and Territories.

Former Yugoslavia

It is assumed, pending notice of new legislation, that protection continues in Bosnia-Herzegovina, Croatia, Macedonia, Montenegro, Serbia and Slovenia as outlined in the main text Synopsis entry for Yugoslavia. Accordingly, these territories are each entered separately in the Synopsis of Laws, under their respective paragraph numbers; the relevant entries are also made in paragraphs 7B.21 (performers: level of protection), 7B.22 (performers: duration), Lists I and II, and the Chart and Index of Countries and Territories. However, in view of the present situation, such listings must not be taken as purporting to represent the prevailing legal or constitutional status of any part of the former Yugoslavia.

Albania

— Law on Author's Right, No. 7564 of May 19, 1993   21.20

It is reported that the Law on Author's Right, No. 7564 of May 19, 1993 establishes protection of authors at the standard required by the Berne Convention, and that there are special provisions concerning performers and broadcasting of records, with civil and criminal remedies for infringement of rights. Consequently, when details are to hand, it may be necessary to revise the main text Synopsis entry as to level, ambit and scope of protection: see *GRUR Int.* 1993, 94; *IIC* 1993, 291.

Convention membership

Albania has acceded to the WIPO Convention, with effect from June 30, 1992: see *Copyright* 1992, 127.
    Albania has acceded to the Berne Convention (Paris text 1971) with effect from March 6, 1994: see *Copyright* 1994, 22.

Convention membership

Insert the Convention membership abbreviations:
B (P), W.

[January 1994]

Angola   (New entry)

— Law on Author's Right, No. 4/90 of March 10, 1990 (*Copyright* 1992, March)   21.60

Literary, dramatic, musical and artistic works: Level I(m) protection by author's right (50 years p.m.a.).

Cinematographic works: Level I(m) protection by author's right for producer, notwithstanding rights of contributors (director and authors of the plot, adaptation, sequences, dialogues and music, in their individual contributions) (50 years p.m.a.).

Convention membership

W.

Remedies and penalties

In addition to civil liability, infringement of rights is punishable by imprisonment, together with a fine of up to 100,000 Kz. (arts. 32 and 36).

[January 1994]

Argentina

Phonograms

21.90 For details of the legislative provisions concerning phonograms, and a summary of the secondary use remuneration system, see note by Millé, A. in [1992] *EIPR*, D-153.

Convention membership

Argentina has ratified the Rome Convention, without reservations, with effect from March 2, 1992: see *Copyright* 1992, 29.
 Argentina has become a member of the Audiovisual Works Registration Treaty: see paragraph 7.49.

Add to the Convention membership abbreviations:
R. See also paragraph 7.49 (AWR Treaty).

[January 1994]

Armenia (New entry)

22.00 Pending notice of new legislation affecting the situation (see para. 21.01, Republics which formed part of the U.S.S.R. on May 31, 1991) it is assumed that protection continues as it was understood to be under the law applying before May 31, 1991, and the following synopsis is on that basis.

Literary, dramatic, musical and artistic works: Level I(m) protection by author's right (25 years p.m.a.).

Audiovisual works: Level I(m) protection by author's right (exploitation rights to producer) (25 years p.m.a.).

Convention membership

Clarification of application of U.C.C. membership is awaited. Armenia has confirmed its membership of the WIPO Convention, with effect from April 22, 1993: see *Copyright* 1993, 29.

W. See also paragraph 20.12 (Satellites).

[January 1994]

Australia

— Copyright Amendment Act 1991

Parallel import of books

The Copyright Amendment Act 1991 introduces provisions restricting in certain cases the copyright owner's powers to prevent import of legitimately produced copies, with different rules for works first published in Australia, and those first published overseas. Introduction of similar rules concerning copies of sound recordings has been under consideration, but no legislation has yet been adopted in this connection. For comment, see [1992] *EIPR* D-22.

Blank tape payments

In *Australian Tape Manufacturers Assn. Ltd. and Others v. Commonwealth of Australia* 176 C.L.R. 480, 112 A.L.R. 53, the High Court of Australia held (by a majority of four to three) that the provisions of the Law amending the Copyright Act 1968 (namely of Part Vc as inserted by the Copyright Amendment Act 1989) and establishing a system of payments on blank tapes, imposed a tax and were invalid, since they did not comply with the Constitution's requirements in respect of laws which levy tax.

It remains to be seen whether the Government will consider the reintroduction of the system in a manner which will conform to the constitutional requirements as declared by the High Court.

Convention membership

Australia became a party to the Satellites Convention on October 26, 1990.

Australia has acceded to the Rome Convention, with effect from September 30, 1992: see *Copyright* 1992, 301. The accession was accompanied by a number of reservations, including one under Article 16(1)(a), *i.e.* that Australia would not apply Article 12. The Copyright Act 1968 recognises the exclusive right of the maker of a protected sound recording to cause the recording to be heard in public, or to broadcast the recording, subject to provisions concerning payment of equitable remuneration (ss.85, 89, 108–109). It is thought that the Australian Government may have concluded that certain provisions of the 1968 Act are not entirely in line with the requirements of the Rome Convention, hence the reservation. Nevertheless, the reservation appears to be anomalous, both in view of the recognition of the principle of Article 12 in Australian law, and the fact that Australia voted for Article 12 at the Rome Convention Conference, 1961: see main text paragraph 7A.10.

Add to the Convention membership abbreviations:
RrX. See also paragraph 20.12 (Satellites)

[January 1994]

Austria

22.60 The texts of the Amendment Laws 1988 No. 601 and 1989 No. 612 are published in *Copyright* 1993, October.

Rental

Rental and lending rights for authors, performers and producers have been specifically introduced into the Austrian Law by the Amending Law UrhRG Nov. 1993: see paragraph 20.31.

[January 1994]

Azerbaidjan (New entry)

22.70 Pending notice of new legislation affecting the situation (see para. 21.01, Republics which formed part of the U.S.S.R. on May 31, 1991) it is assumed that protection continues as it was understood to be under the law applying before May 31, 1991, and the following synopsis is on that basis.

Literary, dramatic, musical and artistic works: Level I(m) protection by author's right (25 years p.m.a.).

Audiovisual works: Level I(m) protection by author's right (exploitation rights to producer) (25 years p.m.a.).

Convention membership

Clarification of application of the U.C.C. and WIPO Convention membership is awaited.

[January 1994]

Bahrain (New Entry)

— Decree No. 10/1993, Official Gazette No. 2039 of June 9, 1993.

Literary, dramatic, musical and artistic works: Level I(m) protection by author's right (50 years p.m.a.).

Cinematographic works: Level 1(m) protection by author's right (the producer being the author's representative for the exploitation rights) (50 years).

General comments

The new author's right law in Bahrain represents a marked advance, establishing general protection for the works of authors. However, because, for instance, of the facilities given for the use of works without permission, the standards of the Law do not yet reach those required by the Berne Convention. There is no protection under the Law for performers, phonogram producers or broadcasting organisations, as required by the Rome Convention.

Cabling

Cabling is not specifically mentioned in the 1993 Decree, but it is assumed, subject to confirmation, that such right is included in the general right to transfer the work to the public (art. 6).

Cinematographic works

The authors of the cinematographic work are the author of the scenario, the adapter, the author of the dialogue, the author of specifically composed musical works and the director (if making an intellectual contribution) plus the author of the adapted pre-existing work (art. 22).

Deposit

There is a system of compulsory deposit of copies of works (fine for breach, art. 35).

Convention membership

[...]

Remedies and penalties

Infringement of author's right is punishable by imprisonment up to one year, plus a fine of up to one thousand dinars, or either. Recidivism within three years is punishable by the maximum penalty (not specified).

[January 1994]

Belarus (New entry: formerly listed as Belorussia)

23.25 Pending notice of new legislation affecting the situation (see para. 21.01, Republics which formed part of the U.S.S.R. on May 31, 1991) it is assumed that protection continues as it was understood to be under the law applying before May 31, 1991, and the following synopsis is on that basis.

Literary, dramatic, musical and artistic works: Level I(m) protection by author's right (25 years p.m.a.).

Audiovisual works: Level I(m) protection by author's right (exploitation rights to producer) (25 years p.m.a.).

Convention membership

Clarification of application of the U.C.C. is awaited.

W.

[January 1994]

Belgium

General comments

23.30 The Law of July 27, 1953 provides for the direct application of the Berne Convention in Belgium, so that Belgians and other Berne Union rightowners may claim any protection provided by the Berne Convention (in the version by which Belgium is bound) where this is more favourable than that provided by the national statute on author's rights. Cinematographic works are thus protected in Belgium, even through the national statute (having been passed in 1886) does not mention them.

As to new law, see Preface.

E.C. Directives

It is anticipated that legislation will be introduced to implement the provisions of E.C. Directives 92/100 (rental and lending rights, and related rights), 93/83 (satellite broadcasting and cable retransmission), and 93/98 (term of protection), in so far as existing Belgian law needs to be revised in this connection (*c.f.* para. 7.51, and see para. 20.20).

[January 1994]

Bolivia

The main text entry is replaced by the following, in consequence of the adoption of a new author's right law in 1992.

— Law No. 1322 of April 13, 1992 (*Copyright* 1993, June)

Literary, dramatic, musical and artistic works: Level I(m) protection by author's right (50 years p.m.a.).

Performances: Level I(m) protection by related right for performer (50 years).

Phonograms: Level I protection by related right for producer (50 years).

Cinematographic works: Level I(m) protection by author's right (exploitation rights to producer) (50 years, art. 19): see below.

Broadcasts: Protected under the 1992 Law.

General comments

Terminology

The rights granted to performers, phonogram producers and broadcasting organisations are termed "*derechos conexos*": *cf.* main text paragraph 5.09.

Article 5(ñ) provides that "cinematographic work and videogram" means the fixation on material support of moving images, with or without sound.

Performer's rights

The performer is granted the right to authorise or prohibit the fixation, reproduction, communication to the public, transmission or any other form of use of his performance. The interpretative artist (*artista intérprete*) is granted "moral rights" of identification, maintenance of integrity of the performance and preservation of reputation, for life, plus (with exercise by heirs) 20 years after death (art. 53). The stage director and the orchestra director exercise the rights (art. 53).

Producer's rights

The producer's right to authorise public communication specifically includes "emission by satellite, or any other method of use" (art. 54).

Remuneration for public communication

As well as granting exclusive rights to authorise public communication, the Law incorporates the provisions of Article 12 of the Rome Convention, establishing the rights of performers and phonogram producers to receive equitable remuneration for broadcasting and public performance of phonograms, to be shared equally in default of other agreement (art. 55; see also art. 56).

Rights in cinematographic works

The patrimonial rights in the cinematographic work are, except for contrary stipulation, granted to the producer, to whom the exploitation rights of the authors are deemed as ceded by the production contract (arts. 30 and 43). The director has the moral rights over the cinematographic work, without prejudice to the rights of the various authors and performers, as to their respective contributions (art. 40).

The co-authors of the cinematographic work are the authors of the plot (*argumento*), the adaptation, the script, and the musical works created especially for the production, and the director (art. 41).

Rental

Phonogram producers are granted the rental right (art. 54): see paragraph 20.31.

Convention membership

Bolivia has acceded to the Berne Convention (Paris text 1971), with effect from November 4, 1993: see *Copyright* 1993, 178.

Bolivia has acceded to the Rome Convention, with effect from November 24, 1993: see *Copyright* 1994, 22.

B (P), U (P), R, W.

Remedies and penalties

The 1992 Law contains an extensive list of offences, including unauthorised reproduction of and import, distribution, etc., of illicit copies of phonograms and videograms, false naming of authors, performers, producers, etc., the sanctions being those provided by the Penal Code, article 362: remedies under the 1992 Law include destruction, seizure, etc., of unlawful copies (arts. 65–70).

[January 1994]

Bosnia–Herzegovina (New entry)

Pending notice of new legislation affecting the situation (see para. 21.01, Former Yugoslavia) it is assumed that protection continues as outlined in main text paragraph 47.60, Yugoslavia, and the following synopsis is on that basis.

Literary, dramatic, musical and artistic works: Level I(m) protection by author's right (50 years p.m.a.).

Performances: Level IIx(m) protection by performer's right (20 years).

Cinematographic works: Level I(m) protection by author's right (50 years p.m.a.) (last surviving author).

Convention membership

Bosnia–Herzegovina has confirmed its membership of the WIPO Convention, the Berne Convention (Paris text 1971), and the Universal Copyright Convention (Geneva text 1952 and Paris text 1971): see *Copyright* 1994, 21.

B (P), U (P), W.

[January 1994]

Brazil

Convention membership

Brazil has ratified the Audiovisual Works Registration Treaty, with effect from June 26, 1993: see paragraph 7.49.

Add to the Convention membership abbreviations:
See paragraph 7.49 (AWR Treaty).

[January 1994]

Bulgaria

24.70   The main text entry is replaced by the following, in consequence of the adoption of a new author's right law in 1993.

— Law on Author's Right and Neighbouring Rights, of June 16, 1993 (entered into force August 1, 1993).

Literary, dramatic, musical and artistic works: Level I(m) protection by author's right (50 years p.m.a.).

Performances: Level I(m) protection by neighbouring right for performer (50 years).

Phonograms: Level I protection by neighbouring right (including "moral" right) for producer (50 years).

Films and other audiovisual works: Level I(m) protection by author's right for director, author of script and director of photography (exploitation rights deemed granted to producer) (50 years).

Broadcasts: Protected under Law of June 16, 1993.

General comments

Cabling

Authorisation for wireless broadcasting of a work includes authorisation for cabling of the work, without separate payment, provided the cabling is simultaneous and unchanged, and takes place within the area for which broadcasting of the work has been authorised (art. 21).

Satellite transmission

Authorisation for wireless broadcasting of a work includes the right to transmit to a satellite, permitting the work to be received through another organisation, provided the receiving organisation has been authorised to broadcast or cable the work, in which case no payment is due from the transmitting organisation (art. 22). Clarification of the precise application of this provision is awaited.

Performer's moral rights

The performer is granted the moral rights of (1) indication of name on use of live or recorded performance, (2) integrity and immutability of his performance (art. 75).

Performer's economic rights

The performer is granted the exclusive right to authorise broadcasting, cabling or sound or video recording of his performance, distribution of such recordings, and public performance, broadcasting and cabling of such recordings (art. 76(1)(2)). Exclusivity contracts may not exceed five years (art. 76(3)). Unless otherwise agreed, the producer is deemed to be granted exploitation rights (including broadcasting and cabling) (art. 76(3)).

Unless otherwise agreed the performer taking part in the making of a film is deemed to have granted exploitation rights in the film (including video rights) to the producer (art. 78).

Artists' group names are to be registered, and may then not be used by another group (duration of right: 10 years) (art. 82).

Producer's "moral" right

The phonogram producer has the right to indication of his name on his recordings.

Producer's economic rights

The phonogram producer has the exclusive right to authorise the reproduction and distribution of his recording, the import and export of copies of his recording (whether made legally or not), and public performance, broadcasting and cabling of his recording (art. 86).

Sound recordings

For a general summary of the protection of sound recordings in Bulgaria, see Dietz, A. in [1993] *Ent. L.R.* 99.

Remuneration for secondary use

The rate of remuneration for performers and phonogram producers in respect of the broadcasting, cabling or public communication of performances and published phonograms is set out in separate provisions. The remuneration is to be divided equally between the performers and the producers (arts. 77 and 88).

Films and other audiovisual works

The provisions of the previous Law of 1951 (art. 16), under which the right in the film belonged to the producer, has been replaced by a system of presumption of cession.

The author's rights in the film or other audiovisual work belong to the director, the author of the script, and the director of photography (art. 62(1)). The authors of the music, dialogue, pre-existing work, scenery, costumes, etc., have separate author's rights in their works (art. 62(2)).

By virtue of the contract between the film authors and the producer, the producer is, unless otherwise agreed, granted exclusive authorisation rights in the film, with obligation to pay remuneration to the authors (art. 63(1)(2)).

Blank tape

The previous system instituted by Decree No. 19, February 13, 1991, under which remuneration is due to authors, performers and producers, by means of payment on blank audio and video tape, is continued in the 1993 Law: see paragraph 20.28.

Rental

Authors, performers and phonogram producers are granted rental rights: see paragraph 20.31.

Convention membership

B (P), U (P), W.

Remedies and penalties

In addition to the rightowner's civil remedies of damages, seizure, etc., in respect of infringement (arts. 94 and 95), penalties for infringing reproduction, distribution, performance etc. are established at fines ranging from 20,000 to 200,000 leva, or, on second or subsequent conviction within one year, a fine from 100,000 to 500,000 leva; for systematic infringements the shop, studio, etc., may be closed from three to six months (art. 97). The fines are to be expended solely for cultural development and protection of rights, as determined by the Council of Ministers (art. 98(4)).

[The above synopsis is based on the translation provided by Law Firm Arsis, 15 Tsarigradsko Chausse Blvd., Entr. B, 6th floor, 1220 Sofia, Bulgaria. Phone/fax +359 2 445.553.]

[January 1994]

Canada

25.30 The Copyright Act as amended to December 31, 1989 has been published in *Copyright* 1992, June. A number of amendments have been made to that version of the Act by the following legislation.

Synopsis of Laws, Charts, etc.   25.30

— Integrated Circuit Topography Act 1990, c.37
— Miscellaneous Statute Law Amendment Act 1992, c.1
— Intellectual Property Law Improvement Act 1993, c.15
— An Act to amend the Copyright Act 1993, c.23.
— North American Free Trade Agreement Implementation Act 1993, c.44.

All the amendments to the Copyright Act effected by this legislation are in force as at January 15, 1994. For the texts of the principal Act and these amendments, in English and French, see Gendreau, Y. and MacKaay, E., *Canadian Legislation on Intellectual Property* (Carswell, 1993).

In consequence of the amendments, the synopsis entries in the main text for sound recordings (records) and cinematograph productions should read as follows.

Sound recordings *(records)*: Level IV protection by copyright for maker of the record (50 years).

Cinematographs: Level I protection by copyright for authors (50 years (p.m.a. in certain cases)).

In the following, some aspects of the Act, as so amended, are considered.

Cinematograph productions and cinematographs

It would appear that, as a result of the amendments introduced since 1989, the general situation as to the protection of cinematographic material is as follows:

(1) *Cinematograph productions*

Before the amendments effected by the Act 1993, c.44, section 22 provided that "dramatic work" included "any cinematograph production where the arrangement or acting form or the combination of incidents represented give the work an original character". Thus, a film such as *Gone with the Wind* was protected as a dramatic work, or as a series of photographs, independently of the protection in the pre-existing work (*e.g.* a novel) (see main text para. 25.30).

By the Act 1993, c.44, the definition of "dramatic work" is changed, but it would appear that the previous protection of the "original character" cinematograph production as a dramatic work, or as a series of photographs, continues, being subsumed in the protection of the cinematograph (see below). The duration of protection of the dramatic work is 50 years p.m.a., of the photographs 50 years (ss.6, 10(1)).

(2) *Cinematographs*

Under the Act 1993, c.44, "cinematograph" includes any work produced by a process analogous to cinematography (with a certain exception as to duration, which will be discussed below). It would appear that the intention is to create a copyright in two types of cinematograph. The first type consists of works "where the arrangement or acting form or the combination of incidents represented give the work an original character", and the second type where the cinematograph does not have an original character of this type. This may be deduced from the amended definition of cinematograph, which excludes "original character" works from the "fixed 50 year" term of protection now specifically provided for cinematographs in section 11.(1), the implication being that "original character" cinematographs retain the period of 50 years p.m.a. protection for the dramatic work involved (50 years for the photographs).

Several questions remain to be clarified in connection with these amendments:

(1) Are all cinematographs protected, irrespective of original input? Clearly, a documentary video with an original input will be protected as a cinematograph. But what about the "holiday video" which contains no original input? The Canadian Act is based on the U.K. Copyright Act 1911, under which only "original" works may be protected (s.1(1)). The same concept is retained in the Canadian Act, which states in section 5(1) that copyright shall subsist in Canada "in every original literary, dramatic, musical and artistic work" if certain conditions are met. It may therefore be argued that cinematographs must be "original" in order to be protected under the Canadian Act, even though the standard of original input may not be high. In this, the Canadian Act would be consistent with its roots, not so far having specifically granted copyright to productions without requiring an input of originality (as did the U.K. Copyright Act 1956 in respect of films and sound recordings: see main text para. 45.70).

(2) Who is the author, or who are the authors, of the cinematograph? It is thought that this question may be answered in terms of the persons responsible for the original input, subject to the Act's provisions as to employee's works (s.13(3)).

(3) Are the photographs which constitute the cinematograph separately protected? It would seem, on the analogy of the previous situation, that the cinematograph will be protected as such, either for 50 years p.m.a. in the case of "original character" productions, or 50 years in the case of other cinematographs (s.11.(1)), and that the constituent photographs will be separately protected.

Telecommunication and network transmissions

In *Performing Rights Organisation of Canada Ltd. et al v. CTV Television Network Ltd. et al* (1993) 46 C.P.R. 3d 343 (Canadian Fed. Ct. of Appeal) it was held that, in regard to transmission by a television network to its affiliated stations by satellite (the stations then broadcasting to the public):

(1) The transmission was not a performance of musical works in public, there being no graphic reproduction of the work, but rather communication of a performance of the work rather than the work.
(2) The transmission was not a broadcast.
(3) The network was not a retransmitter within the meaning of the Copyright Act.
(4) The network did not authorise public performance of the works in its network programming: it facilitated, but did not authorise.

This case is to be compared with *Canadian Cable Television Association v. Copyright Board et al* (1993) 46 C.P.R. 359 (Canadian Fed. Ct. of Appeal) which concerned CCTA transmission of service programmes to subscribers by electrical signals over a closed network service. The defendant alleged that the transmissions were not public performances of musical works, nor a communication of such works to the public.

Section 3(1) of the Canadian Copyright Act as amended includes in copyright the sole right to perform the work in public, and, in relation to a literary, dramatic, musical or artistic work, also includes the sole right to communicate the work to the public by telecommunication (s.3(1)(f)).

The questions were therefore whether the transmissions constituted: (a) public performance, or (b) communication to the public by telecommunication (or both).

As to (a), the Court, in an interesting departure from the previous understanding of the law, overruled the decision in *Canadian Admiral Corp. Ltd. v. Rediffusion Inc.* (1954) 20 C.P.R. 75, [1954] Ex.C.R. 382, and took the view that radio and television broadcasts amount to performances in public when received in private homes (*cf.* main text para. 45.70(c)(ii), Sound recordings). The appellant was also held to have authorised the public performance.

As to (b), the Court held that the appellant did not communicate musical works to the public within the meaning of section 3(1)(f) of the Copyright Act, applying the earlier decision of the Supreme Court in *CAPAC v. CTV Television Network Ltd.* [1968] S.C.R. 676, (1968) 55 C.P.R. 2d 132.

It should be noted that the decisions related to the previous definition of musical work, as contained in section 2 of the Copyright Act before amendment, and referring to a musical work as being "printed, reduced to writing or otherwise graphically produced or reproduced". The Court, in line with earlier findings, held that such graphic representations could not be communicated by cable. This aspect of the judgments must now be viewed in the light of the 1993 amendment to the Act (1993, c.44) which simply describes a musical work as "any work of music or musical composition, with or without words". Clearly a musical work can be communicated by cable according to this definition. The Act has also been amended (s.3(1.4)) to make network operators liable for their transmissions to other persons, in certain circumstances. Section 3(4) as introduced by the Act 1993, c.44, provides that in respect of the sole right to perform the work in public (s.3(1)), the act of communicating a work to the public by telecommunication does not constitute the act of performing the work in public, or authorising such performance. Thus the right to communicate the work to the public by telecommunication (s.3(1)(f)) is clearly separated from the right to perform the work in public.

Copyright in records

Section 5(4) is amended by the Act 1993, c.44, to provide that copyright in records means the sole right: (a) to reproduce the record in any material form, (b) to publish the record, if it is unpublished, and (c) to rent out the record. Canadian law has not yet reintroduced the performing right in records, but the matter will no doubt continue to be the subject of consideration.

In relation to ownership of copyright in records, section 11 is amended by the Act 1993, c.44, to provide that the maker of the contrivance is deemed to be its author: this is a modernising provision, replacing the previous wording (taken from the U.K. Copyright Act 1911), according to which the person who was the owner of the original plate was deemed to be the author of the contrivance. Nevertheless, the amended text continues to recognise that the maker of the contrivance, and thus its author, can be a body corporate. The record must, it is thought, have an original input to be protected (see above); the common law system has no difficulty in accepting that this input may be effected by a producing company. It may be that, eventually, the Canadian law will bridge the difficulty in nomenclature by granting "related rights" where originality is not a criterion, thus preserving in English and French texts the distinction between "copyright" and "related rights" on the one hand, and "*droit d'auteur*" and "*droit voisins*" on the other. A similar development could take place in the United States, where a work must be original to be protected, as in Canada. In sum, the final pattern may be one in which "copyright" is reserved for productions with an original input (albeit minimal), while related rights are granted to productions where originality is not a criterion, such as performances and broadcasts. See comment in [1994] *EIPR* D-5.

Rental

Under the 1993 amendments, rental rights are granted to authors of computer programs and makers of records: see paragraph 20.31.

[The assistance of Dr. Ysolde Gendreau in providing material for this section is gratefully acknowledged.]

[January 1994]

Chile

25.90 — Law No. 19.166 of September 9, 1992 (duration, phonogram producer's rights)

Consequent upon the amendments introduced by the 1992 Law, the Synopsis of Laws entry in the main text for performances and phonograms should be amended to read as follows:

Performances: Level I(m) protection by performer's right (50 years).

Phonograms: Level Ix protection by producer's right (50 years). The 1992 Law amends the principal Law (17.336/1970) in a number of respects, including the following.

Duration of protection

The general period of protection for authors' works is extended to 50 years p.m.a., and for performances and phonograms to 50 years (1992, arts. 1(1)(3), 9 and 10).

Phonogram producers' rights

Article 67 of the 1970 Law is amended to provide specifically that the remuneration for broadcasting and public communication of records is to be paid both to the performers and to the phonogram producers (1992, art. 8). Thus the phonogram producers now have a statutory right to the remuneration, as distinct from the contractual right to which reference is made in the main text under the heading, Performers' remuneration: sharing.

The remuneration under article 67 of the 1970 Law as amended is to be shared 50/50 between the performers and the phonogram producers. The new law lays down the shares to be paid to the various categories of performers (soloists, conductors, musicians, etc.).

Rental

The phonogram producer's rights under article 68 of the 1970 Law are extended to include the rights of authorising or prohibiting lending and rental and other uses of the phonogram, as well as reproduction (1992, art. 1(9)): see paragraph 20.31.

Cabling

While cabling is not specifically mentioned in the 1970 Law, it is assumed that, by reason of the reference to "communication to the public", some or all aspects of the cabling right are included in the rights granted to authors, performers and phonogram producers.

Convention membership

Chile has ratified the Audiovisual Works Registration Treaty, with effect from December 29, 1993: see *Copyright* 1993, 244, and paragraph 7.49.

Add to the Convention membership abbreviations: See para. 7.49
(AWR Treaty). [January 1994]

China

Legislative instruments

26.00 The relevant legislative instruments are as follows:

(1) Law of September 7, 1990 (translation: *Copyright* 1991, February) (general law on protection of works, performances, etc: see main text para. 26.00).

(2) Implementing Regulations of May 24, 1991 (translations: *WIPR* 1991, 191; *Copyright* 1991, November) (general regulations for implementing the 1990 Law: see main text para. 26.00).

(3) The Computer Software Regulations (translation: IP Asia, July 4, 1991, 22, with commentary by David B. Kay).

(4) Rules for the Registration of Protectible Software 1992.

(5) International Copyright Treaties Implementing Rules of September 25, 1992 (entered into force September 30, 1992) (translations: [1992] *EIPR* D-231; *WIPR* 1992, 325, with note; *Copyright* 1993, April). The Rules are analysed and described by Gao Linghan in *IIC* 1993, 475, with particular reference to the implementation of the Berne Convention in China. See also Chengsi Zheng in *Copyright World* December 1992/January 1993, 33.

(6) The relevant provisions of the General Principles of Civil Law 1986.

By virtue of the increased protection afforded by the Implementing Rules 1991, and it being understood that the rights enjoyed by Chinese citizens and foreigners may not at present be identical, the synopsis of protection is as follows.

Literary, dramatic, musical and artistic works: Level I(m) protection by "work right" for author (50 years p.m.a.).

Performances: Level II protection by performer's right (50 years).

Sound recordings: Level I protection by producer's right (50 years).

Cinematographic, television and video works: Level I(m) protection by "work right" (50 years).

Video recording: Level I protection by producer's right (50 years).

Broadcasts: Protected under Law of September 7, 1990.

General comments

The 1990 Law, the implementing Regulations 1991 and the Implementing Rules 1992 must be read together in order to form a picture of the current provisions of Chinese law in this area. Clearly, the law is in a state of development, as the provisions are extended to meet the requisites of international relations. Despite its complexities, the overall picture is one of a country having accepted or moving towards full recognition of the principles of the Berne 1971, Rome and Phonograms Conventions. At present, in the progress towards achieving this position, the foreign author, performer or producer may be more favourably treated than the Chinese citizen. It is unlikely that such a state of affairs will long continue: "water finds its own level".

In the following, what is understood to be the present position as regards the protection of works in general, and of sound and video recordings is summarised.

Protected works

Article 2 of the 1990 Law provides that the following categories of works enjoy protection under the Law:

(a) Works of Chinese citizens, legal entities, or entities without legal personality, whether such works are published or not.
(b) Works of foreigners first published in China.
(c) Foreigners' works first published outside China and eligible for protection under a bilateral or multilateral treaty to which China is a party.

Article 3 of the Implementing Rules 1992 defines "International copyright treaties" as:

(a) the Berne Convention, and
(b) bilateral agreements relating to copyright which China has concluded with foreign countries.

Article 4 of the Implementing Rules 1992 defines certain categories of foreign works (hereinafter called "foreign protected works"), namely (in summary):

(1) works of which the author is a national or permanent resident of a country party to international copyright treaties;
(2) works which do not fall under (1), but which have been first published or published simultaneously in a country party to international copyright treaties;
(3) works created on commission, of which the owner of the copyright is a joint venture enterprise, a cooperative enterprise or an enterprise with sole foreign investment.

It will be noted that (1) and (2) refer to works with a foreign element, and (3) apparently refers to local productions with a foreign element.

Authors of foreign protected works enjoy the rights granted to authors under the 1990 Law, and the Implementing Rules 1992 confirm the terms of protection in respect of such works (arts. 5–7; *cf.* arts. 20 and 21 of the 1990 Law).

Protection of sound recordings

The general situation appears to be as follows.

(1) *Rights accorded to producers of sound recordings*

(i) *The 1990 Law* Article 39 of the 1990 Law provides that the sound recording producer has the right to authorise the reproduction and distribution of such recordings: by implication, the producer also has the right to receive remuneration for the commercial broadcasting of such recordings (art. 43; see main text para. 26.00).

(ii) *The Implementing Regulations 1991* Article 5 of the Implementing Regulations of May 24, 1991 defines the means of exploitation of works, and includes renting in the definition of "distribution". Since the sound recording producer has the distribution right, it is thought that article 39 of the 1990 Law can be interpreted as meaning that the producer has the rental right (the author also having the rental right: see para. 20.31).

(2) *Entitled producers under the 1990 Law and Implementing Regulations 1991*

The 1990 Law does not specifically define the producers who are entitled to benefit from the protection granted. In so far as sound recordings are analogous to "works", then by virtue of article 2 of the 1990 Law the following categories of producer will enjoy protection:

(a) producers who are Chinese citizens, legal entities or entities without legal personality, whether the recording is published or not;
(b) producers who are foreigners, and who first publish the recording in China;
(c) producers of recordings made by foreigners and eligible for protection by virtue of bilateral or multilateral treaties to which China is a party.

In addition, article 47 of the Implementing Regulations 1991 provides that audio recordings produced and distributed in the territory of China by foreign producers are protected by the Law.

Thus far the protection does not cover the foreign producer who has not produced or first published the recording in China, and who is not covered by article 2 of the 1990 Law, or article 47 of the Implementing Regulations 1991. This lacuna is filled by the Implementing Rules 1992 (see below).

(3) *Rights accorded to foreign producers of sound recordings under the Implementation Rules 1992*

Article 18 of the Implementing Rules 1992 provide that certain provisions of the Rules also apply to sound recordings, namely:

(a) article 5: term of protection;

Synopsis of Laws, Charts, etc.   26.00

(b) article 12: public performance right;
(c) article 14: exclusive rental right;
(d) article 15: importation rights;
(e) article 17: recordings protected in country of origin.

It seems clear that this extended protection is in relation to foreign sound recordings, so that, at present, foreign sound recording producers may enjoy a greater protection than Chinese producers.

Video recordings

It would appear that, in so far as foreign video recordings constitute works, a separate right of public performance is granted, thus increasing the protection from Level II (as shown in the main text) to Level I (see Implementing Rules 1992, art. 12).

The Rules do not mention a separate rental right in respect of foreign video recordings, but it is assumed that such works are covered by article 14 of the Implementing Rules 1992 (rental rights in respect of foreign works).

Increased levels of protection

It will be noted that, as compared with the Synopsis of Laws in main text paragraph 26.00, the level of protection for sound recordings is advanced to Level I from II, this being due to the extension of the authorisation rights (at least of entitled foreign producers) to cover public performance.

Performers, however, apparently do not yet enjoy rights concerning the public performance (as distinct from broadcasting; see the 1990 Law, art. 43), and thus performances retain Level II protection.

Outstanding questions

Among the outstanding questions arising in respect of the current Chinese legislation are the following:

(1) Are sound and video recordings protected only if they constitute works, in the sense that they result from creative input or investment of skill and labour?
(2) Are there separate rights in sound and video recordings which do not constitute "works", in the sense of (1) above? If so, what is the content of such rights?

Rental

Authors and phonogram producers have rental rights: see paragraph 20.31.

Convention membership

China has joined the Berne Convention, with effect from October 15, 1992 (see *Copyright* 1992, 145). China avails itself of the facilities provided for in Articles II and III of the Appendix to the Paris text 1971.

China has acceded to the Geneva text 1952 and Paris text 1971 of the Universal Copyright Convention, by instrument deposited on July 30, 1992: see *UNESCO Cop. Bull.* 1993, XXVII/1/5, 14.

China has acceded to the Phonograms Convention, with effect from April 30, 1993: see *Copyright* 1993, 50.

Add to the Convention membership abbreviation:
B (P), U(P), P.

[The author is grateful to Qui Anman for his comments on this section.]
[January 1994]

Colombia

26.50 — Amending Law No. 44 of February 4, 1993 (duration, administration societies, record performing rights administration, remedies and penalties)

Duration of protection

The 1993 Law amends article 29 of the 1982 Law and provides that the period of protection for performers and phonogram producers is as follows:

— if the right owner is a natural person: 80 years p.m.a.;
— if the right owner is a legal entity: 50 years from publication.

However, no similar provision is applied in regard to cinematographic works, which therefore retain the previous period of protection: 80 years p.m.a. where the right owner is a natural person, 30 years from publication where the rightowner is a legal entity (see arts. 27 and 96 of the 1982 Law). The question therefore arises whether the 1982 Law, in so far as the rights of producers of cinematographic works are limited to 30 years, is in conformity with the Berne Convention, Paris text 1971, Article 7(1)(2).

The administration of the record performing right

The 1993 Law (art. 69) amends the 1982 Law to provide that remuneration for broadcasting and public communication of phonograms shall be paid through an administration society, for equal distribution to the performers and phonogram producers.

Synopsis of Laws, Charts, etc.

Rights of performers

Correction. In the main text Synopsis, paragraph 26.50, the indication for moral rights, (m), should be added to the Performances line (to read now "Level Ix(m) protection by neighbouring right for performer"), and deleted from the Phonograms line.

Remedies and penalties

In general, the 1993 Law extends the civil remedies available and increases the penalties for infringement of the rights granted by the 1982 Law (*e.g.* two to five year's imprisonment plus fine, for unauthorised reproduction: in serious cases, these limits may be increased (arts. 51–53)). The police are given extensive powers to deal with illegal activities involving infringement (art. 54).

[January 1994]

Croatia (New entry)

Pending notice of new legislation affecting the situation (see para. 21.01, Former Yugoslavia), it is assumed that protection continues as outlined in main text paragraph 47.60, Yugoslavia, and the following synopsis is on that basis. It is reported that the amended 1978 Law has been taken into the law of Croatia (with minor amendments) by a specific enactment: see Krneta, S. in *GRUR Int.* 1993, 717, particularly footnote 64.

Literary, dramatic, musical and artistic works: Level I(m) protection by author's right (50 years p.m.a.).

Performances: Level IIx(m) protection by performer's right (20 years).

Cinematographic works: Level I(m) protection by author's right (50 years p.m.a.: last surviving author).

Convention membership

Croatia has declared that it will continue to apply (*inter alia*) the WIPO Convention and the Berne Convention (Paris text 1971) (see *Copyright* 1992, 18) and the Satellites Convention (see *Copyright* 1993, 254). Croatia has confirmed its membership of the Universal Copyright Convention (Paris text 1971) by declaration of July 1, 1992: see *UNESCO Cop. Bull.* 1993, XXVII/1/4, 14.

B (P), U(P), W. See also paragraph 20.12 (Satellites).

[January 1994]

Cyprus

27.50 A number of amendments to the Law of December 3, 1976 are introduced by the Copyright (Amendment) Act 1993, among which are the following.

Duration of protection of sound recordings

The 1993 Law increases the term of protection of sound recordings from 20 to 50 years.

Definition of "broadcast"

The definition is amended to provide that "broadcast" means a sound or visual broadcast by wireless telegraphy or wire, or both, and includes any method of receiving or transmitting by satellite or through cable system.

The Cypriot Law is therefore one of those which use the term "broadcast" to cover both transmission by wireless and by cable: *cf.* main text paragraph 7.25.

Definition of "copyright"

The 1993 Law amends the principal Act by providing in section 7(1) that, subject to various specified exceptions, copyright in a scientific, literary, musical or artistic work, cinematographic film or photograph consists of the exclusive rights of reproduction, sale, rental, distribution, lending, advertising, exhibiting in public, communication to the public, broadcasting, translation, adapting and any other arrangement, of the whole work or any substantial part thereof.

Rental

A rental right in respect of scientific, literary, musical or artistic works, cinematograph films and photographs is introduced by the 1993 amendment of section 7(1): see paragraph 20.31.

Authorisation stickers

A system of affixation of special stickers indicating that the copy of the audio recording, cinematograph film or computer program is duly authorised is introduced by section 14A of the 1993 Law.

Bibliography

See Keane, T.M., "The new Copyright Law in Cyprus" *Copyright World* 1994, February, 31.

Convention membership

Cyprus has acceded to the Phonograms Convention, with effect from September 30, 1993: see *Copyright* 1993, 120.

Add to Convention membership abbreviations:
P.

Remedies and penalties

The Copyright (Amendment) Act 1993 introduces the right, in any infringement action, of delivery up to the owner of the copyright, who is deemed to be the owner of all copies which appear to the Court to be infringing copies (s.13(4), as amended).

The penalties for offences are increased, according to the particular offence involved, to a fine of up to £1,500 or imprisonment up to two years, or both, and in the case of any second or subsequent conviction, a fine of up to £2,000 or imprisonment up to three years, or both.

[January 1994]

Czechoslovakia

The Synopsis of Laws entry for Czechoslovakia in the main text is superseded by the entries for the Czech Republic (see para. 27.70), and the Slovak Republic (see para. 42.65).

Phonograms: It should be noted that the level of protection for phonograms under Law No. 35 of March 25, 1965 is "I" not "Ix", the producer having the exclusive rights to authorise recording, broadcasting and communication to the public of phonograms, and in addition the right to compensation for the consent given in exercise of these rights (art. 45(2)(3)).

[January 1994]

Czech Republic (New entry)

The main text entry for Czechoslovakia (para. 27.60) is replaced by the following, in relation to the Czech Republic. The entry is made on the basis that the Czech Republic continues to apply the following legislation:

— Law No. 35 of March 25, 1965, as modified and amended by Law No. 89 of March 28, 1990, and Federal Law No. 468 of November 1, 1991 (Czech and Slovak Republics)
— Decree No. 115/1991 of March 15, 1991 (Ministry of Culture, Czech Republic)

Literary, dramatic, musical and artistic works: Level I(m) protection by author's right (50 years p.m.a.).

Performances: Level Ix protection by performer's right (50 years).

Phonograms: Level I protection by producer's right (50 years).

Cinematographic works: Level I(m) protection by author's right exercised by producer (50 years).

Broadcasts: protected under the Law of March 25, 1965.

General comments

There are a number of points remaining for clarification following the separation of the Czech Republic and the Slovak Republic into two separate States, as from January 1, 1993, and it may, in consequence, be necessary to amend this entry accordingly when further details are obtained.

Broadcasting

Article 16 of the 1965 Law, which permitted broadcast transmission of works, subject to remuneration of the author, has been amended by the Federal Law of November 1, 1991, removing the compulsory licence and providing that simultaneous, integral and unchanged cabling of broadcasts is considered part of the original broadcast.

Blank tape payment

The former system of payment on blank tape is retained: see paragraph 20.28.

Rental

Authors, performers, phonogram producers and broadcasting organisations have the right to receive remuneration for the rental of recordings of their respective productions: see paragraph 20.31.

Sound recordings

For a general summary of the protection of sound recordings in the Czech Republic, see Dietz, A. in [1993] *Ent. L.R.* 99.

SYNOPSIS OF LAWS, CHARTS, ETC.   27.80

Convention membership

The Czech Republic has confirmed its membership of the Berne Convention (Paris text 1971), the Universal Copyright Convention (Geneva text 1952 and Paris text 1971), the Rome Convention (with reservations) and the Phonograms Convention: see *Copyright* 1993, 17; *Copyright* 1994, p. 23.

The Czech Republic has confirmed its membership of the Audiovisual Works Registration Treaty: see paragraph 7.49.

B (P), U(P), Rr, P, W. See also paragraph 7.49 (AWR Treaty).

[January 1994]

Denmark

— Amending Law No. 338 of May 14, 1992 (blank tape payment)   27.80

For translation of the text of Law No. 158 of May 31, 1961, as amended to June 7, 1989, see Consolidation Law No. 453 of June 23, 1989 (*Copyright* 1991, December). See also *Copyright* 1991, December (legislation on photography; *droit de suite*; storage and use of recordings of radio and TV broadcasts made for educational purposes; collection of remuneration arising under the 1961 Act, article 22a, etc.; work and photograph use remuneration; access by archives libraries, etc.).

Blank tape payment

By the Amending Law of May 14, 1992, a system of payments on blank audio and video tapes has been introduced: see paragraph 20.28.

Film exploitation right

Correction. The reference in main text paragraph 27.80 should be to the right to subtitle (not "subsist") or dub the film in another language.

E.C. Directives

It is anticipated that legislation will be introduced to implement the provisions of E.C. Directives 92/100 (rental and lending rights, and related rights), 93/83 (satellite broadcasting and cable retransmission), and 93/98 (term of protection), in so far as existing Danish law needs to be revised in this connection (*cf.* para. 7.51 and see para. 20.20).

[January 1994]

Ecuador

28.30 — Law No. 161 of July 14, 1992, amending Decree 2821 of August 25, 1978

Remedies and penalties

The amending Law of July 14, 1992 provides for penalties of imprisonment of one to three years, and a fine of five to 20 minimum salaries, for unauthorised reproduction of phonograms or audiovisual recordings, or sale, distribution, rental, etc., of illicit copies. Phonogram and videogram producers are given civil and criminal rights.

[January 1994]

Egypt

28.40 — Amending Law No. 38 of June 4, 1992 (author's rights, penalties)

See also Presidential Decree No. 442/1977 (implementation of Phonograms Convention).

Implementing Regulations are reported to have been adopted in Ministerial Decree No. 162/1993: see *Copyright World* 1993, October, 8.

The Law of June 4, 1992 amends the principal Act (Law No. 354 of June 24, 1954) in the following respects, *inter alia*:

(1) Article 2 (protected works) is reworded and now includes items referring to audio and audiovisual works specially prepared for broadcasting, and to computer programs. It is understood that audio and audiovisual works specially prepared for broadcasting are normally produced by the broadcaster.

(2) Article 20 provides a period of 20 years of protection for computer programs.

Remedies and penalties

Under the Law of June 4, 1992, infringement of rights is punishable with imprisonment and fine from LE 5,000 to LE 10,000, or either penalty (art. 47).

[The author is grateful to Makeen Fouad Makeen for material and comments on this section.]

[January 1994]

El Salvador

28.50 The main text entry is replaced by the following, in consequence of the adoption of a new intellectual property law in 1993.

Synopsis of Laws, Charts, etc.   28.50

— Decree 604 of July 15, 1993

Literary, dramatic, musical and artistic works: Level I(m) protection by author's right (50 years p.m.a.).

Performances: Level I(x)(m) protection by performer's right (50 years): see note below.

Phonograms: Level I(x) protection by producer's right (50 years): see note below.

Cinematographic works: Level I(m) protection for co-authors (exploitation rights to producer) (50 years).

Broadcasts: Protected under Decree 604 of July 15, 1993.

General comments

Cabling

Cable transmission is specifically included within the ambit of the right to communicate the work to the public (arts. 8 and 9(d)).

Performers' rights

Performers are given exclusive rights regarding the fixation, reproduction or communication of their performances to the public, but the communication right does not cover communication by an authorised recording (art. 81). Performers are not specifically granted a right to receive remuneration for the broadcasting or public communication of their performances. Nevertheless El Salvador is obliged to grant such protection as regards foreign recordings, by virtue of Article 12 of the Rome Convention, of which El Salvador is a member (without reservations). Consequently, Level Ix is attributed as regards protection of performances, on the basis of the Rome Convention.

Phonogram producers' rights

Phonogram producers are given an exclusive right regarding reproduction, importation, renting (see below), distribution to the public and any other use of their phonograms. It is assumed, subject to confirmation, that this constitutes Level I protection: in any event, Level Ix protection is attributable in view of El Salvador's membership of the Rome Convention.

Cinematographic works

The authors of the cinematographic work are the director and the authors of the plot, the adaptation, the dialogues, the specially composed music, designs, the cartoons (where animated) and, if applying, the adapted pre-existing work.

Rental

Authors and phonogram producers are granted rental rights: see paragraph 20.31.

Convention membership

El Salvador has acceded to the Berne Convention (Paris text 1971) with effect from February 19, 1993: see *Copyright* 1993, 271.

B (P), U (P), R, P, W.

[January 1994]

Estonia (New entry)

28.60 — Law on Author's Right, of November promulgated 11, 1992 (*Copyright* 1994, February)

Literary, dramatic, musical and artistic works: Level I(m) protection by author's right (50 years p.m.a.).

Performances: Level Ix(m) protection by neighbouring right for performers (50 years).

Phonograms: Level Ix(m) protection by neighbouring right for producer (50 years).

Audiovisual works: Level I(m) protection by author's right (economic rights to producer, unless otherwise agreed) (author's right 50 years p.m.a.; producer's right 50 years).

Broadcasts: Protected under the 1992 Law.

General comments

Of the countries formerly part of the U.S.S.R. (see para. 21.01), Estonia was the first to pass a new law on author's right and neighbouring rights (followed by Latvia and the Russian Federation in 1993). The Estonian Law is notable for the high standard of protection and comprehensive coverage of author's right and neighbouring rights (including rental rights and blank tape payments) which it affords. For the previous history of Estonian law in this field, and background to and commentary on the 1992 Law, see Pisuke H., "Estonia again on the world copyright map" *Copyright World* 1993, March, 24.

Audiovisual works

Article 33 provides that the author or joint authors of the audiovisual work (director, scriptwriter, composer, cameraman and designer) enjoy author's right in the work (*i.e.* moral and economic rights), but the economic rights are transferred to the producer, unless provided otherwise in the contract (no transfer in the case of musical works). The director, scriptwriter and composer, and all others who have contributed to the creation of the audiovisual work can each exercise their economic rights in their respective independent contributions, provided this does not prejudice the use of the work as a whole (art. 33).

Performers' moral rights

Performers have moral rights of "performership", use of name, inviolability of the performance and protection of honour and reputation (art. 66).

Performers' economic rights

The performer's economic rights are in line with those guaranteed by Articles 7 and 12 of the Rome Convention (see main text para. 7B.07). In addition, the performer has a general right regarding use of his performance, and a right to remuneration for such use (art. 67(1)).

Producers' economic rights

The producers' economic rights are in line with those guaranteed by Articles 10 and 12 of the Rome Convention (see main text para. 7.46).

Remuneration for use of phonograms

Article 72 incorporates the principle of Article 12 of the Rome Convention, providing for payment of remuneration (to be shared equally unless otherwise agreed) by performers and producers, in respect of the broadcasting or public communication of phonograms.

Private copying

A system of remuneration (from payments on audio and video recording equipment and tapes, etc.) for private copying is instituted in article 27: see paragraph 20.28.

Rental

Authors and phonogram producers are granted rental rights: see paragraph 20.31.

Convention membership

Estonia has acceded to the WIPO Convention, with effect from February 5, 1994: see *WIPR* 1994, March, 85.

The question of Estonia's membership of the other Convention to which the U.S.S.R. was a party (U.C.C. (Geneva 1952)), is for decision. Estonia became a party to the Berne Convention (Berlin Act 1908) in 1927: the status of the termination of this membership, following Estonia's incorporation in the U.S.S.R. in 1940, remains to be clarified.

W.

Remedies and penalties

Extensive civil remedies are specified as regards infringement of rights, together with civil and criminal liability under the general law (arts. 79–81).

[The above summary is on the basis of an unofficial translation kindly made available through Professor Heiki Pisuke].

[February 1994]

Finland

— Law No. 34 of January 11, 1991, amending Law No. 404 of July 8, 1961 (*Copyright* 1992, April)

See also *Copyright* 1992, April (photographs).
Following the 1991 amendments, the Synopsis of Laws entries for performances and phonograms read as follows:

Performances: Level Ix protection by performer's right (50 years).

Phonograms: Level Ix protection by producer's right (50 years).

General comments

The amending Act of January 11, 1991 introduces a number of important amendments to the 1961 Act, including the following.

Performers' rights

Article 45 is amended to provide: (1) performers' rights over audio or video recording, or broadcast or direct public communication, of live performances (art. 45); (2) increase of the protection period of recorded performances, from 25 to 50 years (art. 45); (3) extension of secondary remuneration rights to public performance for gain (see below).

Producers' rights

Article 46 is amended to extend the term of phonogram producers' exclusive rights to authorise copying of phonograms from 25 to 50 years. Article 47 is amended to extend the secondary remuneration right cover to public performance for gain, as well as broadcasting (see below).

Remuneration for secondary use of phonograms

Under the Finnish Law in force before the 1991 amendment, performers and producers had the right to compensation for the broadcasting, but not public performance, of phonograms. This meant that Finnish law recognised only one of the two secondary uses giving rise to remuneration in accordance with Article 12 of the Rome Convention, *i.e.* broadcasting, but not public performance (in cafés, discotheques, etc.). In this respect the Finnish Law was similar to the previous Swedish Law, which before the amending Law of June 5, 1986 covered only broadcasting in this context (see main text para. 4.60). This limited recognition necessitated the reservations made by Sweden and Finland in accepting Article 12 of the Rome Convention (*i.e.* payment would only be due in respect of broadcasting of phonograms (see *Copyright* 1962, 138; *Copyright* 1983, 282)). Sweden amended its reservation so as to reflect the extension in its Law, indicating that Article 12 would be applied to broadcasting and communication to the public carried out for commercial purposes (see *Copyright* 1986, 382). It may be anticipated that now that Finnish law gives full effect to Article 12, an amendment of Finland's reservation as regards the Article will be made.

Rental

The 1991 amendments introduce a rental right for authors: see paragraph 20.31.

[January 1994]

France

29.30 — Code of Intellectual Property: Law No. 92–597 of July 1, 1992 (*Copyright* 1993, July/August)

See also *Copyright*, 1993, July/August (Law on statutory deposit, No. 92–546 of June 20, 1992).

General comments

The Code of Intellectual Property (Law No. 92–597 of July 1, 1992) (CIP), published in the *Journal Officiel*, July 3, 1992, codifies the Law on author's right, designs and models, patents, trade secrets, semiconductor topographies, plant rights, trade marks and service marks and *appellations d'origine*. The provisions of the Laws of March 11, 1957 and July 3, 1985 are incorporated in the Code (with different article numbers), with some modifications and additions. The basic levels of protection and duration of author's right and neighbouring rights remain unaltered. The numbers of the CIP articles corresponding to those of the 1957 and 1985 Laws mentioned in the main text are given under France in the Table of Legislative Instruments.

Private copying

The system instituted under the 1985 Law is maintained under the CIP: see paragraph 28.20.

Rental

The system instituted under the 1985 Law is maintained under the CIP: see paragraph 20.31.

E.C. Directives

It is anticipated that legislation will be introduced to implement the provisions of E.C. Directives 92/100 (rental and lending rights, and related rights), 93/83 (satellite broadcasting and cable retransmission), and 93/98 (term of protection), in so far as existing French law needs to be revised in this connection (*c.f.* para. 7.51, and see para. 20.20).

[January 1994]

SYNOPSIS OF LAWS, CHARTS, ETC. 30.00

Gambia

Convention membership

Gambia has acceded to the Berne Convention (Paris text 1971), with effect from May 7, 1993: see *Copyright* 1993, 18. 30.00

Add to Convention membership abbreviation:
B (P)

[January 1994]

Georgia (New entry)

Pending notice of new legislation affecting the situation (see para. 21.01, Republics which formed part of the U.S.S.R. on May 31, 1991) it is assumed that protection continues as it was understood to be under the law applying before May 31, 1991, and the following synopsis is on that basis. 30.10

Literary, dramatic, musical and artistic works: Level I(m) protection by author's right (25 years p.m.a.).

Audiovisual works: Level I(m) protection by author's right (exploitation rights to producer) (25 years p.m.a.).

Convention membership

Georgia has confirmed its membership of the WIPO Convention: see *Copyright* 1994, 43.
 Clarification of application of the U.C.C. is awaited.
W. [February 1994]

Germany

— Law of June 9, 1993 (computer programs) 30.20

The Law of June 9, 1993 amends the Author's Right Law 1965 to bring German law in line with E.C. Directive 91/250 (see main text para. 7.51).

National treatment: performers' rights

A publication in a Rome Convention Contracting State, without the performer's consent, fulfils the criteria under Articles 4(b) and 5(1)(c) of the Convention, rendering the performance one which is entitled to national treatment: *Duo Gismonti-Vasconcelos* (LG Munich, May 17, 1991) *GRUR Int.* 1993, 82.

For the application of national treatment to European Union nationals, without discrimination, see *Phil Collins v. IMTRAT*, paragraph 7.38.

Video use of film music

On the complex questions which can arise under national law in determining the rights which apply in the video exploitation of music from cinema film soundtracks, see *"Videoweitauswertung II"*, *GRUR* 1994, 41 (BGH, 1993).

E.C. Directives

It is anticipated that legislation will be introduced to implement the provisions of E.C. Directives 92/100 (rental and lending rights, and related rights), 93/83 (satellite broadcasting and cable retransmission), and 93/98 (term of protection), in so far as existing German law needs to be revised in this connection (*c.f.* para. 7.51, and see para. 20.20).

Unification of Germany

For the sake of completing the reference, it may be noted that as from October 3, 1990 the German Democratic Republic and the Federal Republic of Germany form one sovereign State, bound by the WIPO Convention as "Germany": see *Copyright* 1990, 341.

[January 1994]

Greece

30.50   The main text entry is replaced by the following, in consequence of the adoption of a new intellectual property law in 1993.

— Law No. 2121 of March 3, 1993 (intellectual property, related rights and cultural themes)

Literary, dramatic, musical and artistic works: Level I(m) protection for author by right of intellectual property (70 years p.m.a.).

Performances: Level Ix(m) protection by related right for performer (50 years).

Sound recordings: Level Ix protection by related right for producer (50 years).

Audiovisual works: Level I(m) protection for author (presumed to be the director, art. 9), exploitation rights to producer (subject to contract, art. 34) (70 years p.m.a.).

Audiovisual recordings: Level Ix protection by related right for producer (50 years).

Broadcasts: Protected under the Law of March 3, 1993.

General comments

Terminology

There are a number of interesting features in the terminology adopted in the Greek Law.

The general right encompassed by the Law is one of "intellectual property", which is described as the author's property right (art. 1).

The terms "sound recording", "audiovisual work" and "audiovisual recording" are not literal equivalents of the terms in the Greek text. These may be translated as:

(a) sound recording: "material form of sound";
(b) audiovisual work: "optico-acoustic work";
(c) audiovisual recording: "material form of visual appearance" (*eikóna*).

Cabling

The 1993 Law specifically includes cabling in the ambit of exclusive rights given to authors (art. 3(1)(g)) and performers (art. 46(2)(c)(d)), and of the reasonable remuneration rights of performers and producers (art. 49(1)).

Satellite transmission

Broadcasting by satellite is specifically included in the ambit of the exclusive rights given to authors (art. 3(1)(g)) and performers (art. 46(2)(c)(d)), and of the equitable remuneration rights of performers and producers (art. 49(1)). Third party broadcasting through satellite or otherwise must be authorised (art. 35(2)). Satellite transmissions receivable in Greece must be authorised for broadcast to Greece (art. 35(3)). This would seem to indicate that the licence of the Greek rightowner must be obtained (*cf*. Bogsch theory, main text para. 4.63), subject to the provisions of E.C. Directive 93/83: see paragraph 7.51B.

Computer programs and databases

Computer programs are protected by author's right, where original (*i.e.* the personal intellectual work of the author) (art. 2(1)). There are provisions concerning decompilation, etc. (art. 43).

Databases are protected by author's right where the selection and arrangement of their contents is original (art. 2(2)).

Private copying

Article 18 of the 1993 Law introduces a system of remuneration, based on payments by manufacturers and importers of and dealers in recording devices and tapes, photocopying machines, photocopying paper and computers, for the benefit of authors, performers and producers: see paragraph 20.28.

Rental

The 1993 Law introduces rental rights for authors, performers, producers and broadcasting organisations: see paragraph 20.31.

Performers' exclusive rights

A system under which, subject to contrary agreement, the employer is granted a licence in respect of the use of the performance for the purpose of the employment contract, subject to an unwaivable right to payment, is instituted under article 46(3).

See also Remuneration rights of performers and producers, below.

Remuneration rights of performers and producers

Article 49(1) of the 1993 Law provides that when legitimate sound or audiovisual recordings are used for any form of broadcasting, including satellite or cable transmission, or for public performance, a single reasonable remuneration is to be paid to the performers and the producers. The remuneration is administered collectively, though the performers' right is not assignable (art. 49(1)). The payment is shared 50/50 between performers and producers.

Performers also have a right to reasonable remuneration for the broadcasting of their live performances (art. 49(4)).

Rights in cinematographic works under the 1986 Law

Law No. 1597 of 1986 provided in article 3(1) that the director enjoyed the right in a cinematographic work, without prejudice to the rights of other contributors in their respective intellectual creations: the reference in the main text to the position under the previous Law should be amended accordingly. [Reference provided by Angeliki Ioannidou].

Rights in Audiovisual works under the 1993 Law

Under the 1993 Law, there is a rebuttable presumption that the director is the author of the cinematographic work (art. 9).

In the case of employee's works the employee is the owner of the economic and moral rights, and the employer, subject to agreement to the contrary, is granted only those powers of the economic rights necessary for fulfilling the purpose of the contract (art. 8).

Where the contract between the producer and the author does not provide that the exploitation right is transferred to the producer, the contract effects the transfer to the producer of those exploitation rights necessary for the fulfilment of the purpose of the contract (art. 34).

International Conventions

In general, the 1993 Law applies, subject to the provisions of International Conventions of which Greece is a member. Where no International Convention applies as regards a particular State, the 1993 Law applies, subject to reciprocal protection of subject matter first published or originating in Greece (art. 67(4)).

E.C. Directives

It is anticipated that legislation will be introduced to implement the provisions of E.C. Directives 92/100 (rental and lending rights, and related rights), 93/83 (satellite broadcasting and cable retransmission), and 93/98 (term of protection), in so far as existing Greek law needs to be revised in this connection (*cf.* para. 7.51, and see para. 20.20).

Bibliography

On the background and content of the 1993 Law see Koumantos, G., "The new Greek Law on author's right and neighbouring rights" *RIDA* 159, 204.

Convention membership

Greece has acceded to the Rome Convention, with effect from January 6, 1993: see *Copyright* 1993, 19.

Greece has acceded to the Phonograms Convention, with effect from February 9, 1994.

B(P), U(G), R, P, W. See also paragraph 20.12 (Satellites) and main text paragraph 20.12 (TFE).

Remedies and penalties

The 1993 Law contains special provisions (arts. 59–63) to deal with infringements of rights, including imposition of standards, control systems, application of identification stickers (following Decree), prohibition of unauthorised decoding, etc.

There are statutory confiscation procedures for infringing copies (art. 64), and extensive civil remedies (art. 65).

Criminal penalties for infringement range from imprisonment for up to 10 years (depending on the offence), and fine of up to 20 million drachmas (art. 66).

[The assistance of George Paravantis in the preparation of this synopsis is gratefully acknowledged.]

[January 1994]

Honduras

31.70 — Law on the Intellectual Rights of Phonogram Producers, No. 131–91 of October 22, 1991 (*Copyright* 1992, May)

Term of protection of phonograms

The term of protection under the 1991 Law is 30 years for phonograms produced in Honduras, and, for foreign phonograms, for "the time specified in the laws of the country of registration of the phonogram".

The term runs from the date of first publication.

Remedies and penalties

Article 1 of the 1991 Law provides, as criminal penalties for

(a) unauthorised reproduction, and

(b) import, transportation, sale, rental, etc., of unlawful copies of phonograms,

imprisonment for two to five years, confiscation of unlawful copies and of equipment used for making such copies.

Article 4 provides that the phonogram producer or his legal representative is authorised to bring the appropriate legal actions against infringers.

Article 6 provides that the indemnification to be paid by the infringer to the aggrieved party shall be equal to the selling price of a lawful copy, multiplied by the number of confiscated unlawful copies, with a minimum of the value of 500 copies.

Royalties are also to be paid to the authors and performers out of the indemnification.

Printers must obtain the necessary authorisation from the producer for the printing of sleeves, labels, etc. (art. 5).

Private copying and certain copying for educational purposes are excluded from the Law.

[January 1994]

Hungary

A new law concerning neighbouring rights was adopted on February 8, 1994, together with a resolution concerning membership of the Rome Convention. See Preface.

Sound recordings

For a general summary of the protection of sound recordings in Hungary, see Dietz, A. in [1993] *Ent. L.R.* 99.

Remedies and penalties

By amendment of the Penal Code, dated March 2, 1993, the penalties for infringement of rights of authors, performers, recording producers and broadcasters is punishable, according to the nature of the offence and the extent of damage caused, by imprisonment for up to five years, or fine (maximum reported to be 3.6 million forints).

[February 1994]

Iceland

It is reported that, under the amending Law of May 19, 1992, the term of protection for performances and phonograms is increased to 50 years (from 25 years), and that rental rights are introduced.

[January 1994]

India

— Copyright (Amendment) Ordinance, No. 9 of 1991 (*Copyright* 1992, April)

Duration of protection

The general term of duration of protection for literary, dramatic, musical and artistic works, records and cinematograph films is increased to 60 years (p.m.a. in the case of literary works) by the Copyright (Amendment) Ordinance 1991.

[January 1994]

Ireland

32.60 See also *Copyright* 1992, December (application, proceedings fees, and semiconductor topography rules and regulations).

E.C. Directives

It is anticipated that legislation will be introduced to implement the provisions of E.C. Directives 92/100 (rental and lending rights, and related rights), 93/83 (satellite broadcasting and cable retransmission), and 93/98 (term of protection), in so far as existing Irish law needs to be revised in this connection (*cf.* para. 7.51, and see para. 20.20).

[January 1994]

Isle of Man   (New entry)

32.70 — Copyright Act 1991, c.8

Literary, dramatic, musical and artistic works: Level I(m) protection by copyright for author (50 years p.m.a.).

Sound recordings: Level I protection by copyright for producer (maker) (50 years).

Films: Level I protection by copyright for producer (maker) (moral rights for director) (50 years).

Broadcasts: Protected under Copyright Act 1991.

General comments

Copyright law in the Isle of Man was previously constituted by the extension there of the U.K. Copyright Act 1956 (see main text para. 45.70, Additional notes). The extension of the U.K. 1956 Act to the Isle of Man was revoked by the Copyright (Isle of Man) (Revocation) Order 1992 (S.I. 1992 No. 1306) with effect from July 1,

1992. The Isle of Man now has a separate Copyright Act (1991), which incorporates the provisions of Part I of the U.K. Copyright, Designs and Patents Act 1988 (but not including Part II of the Act, regarding protection of performers).

For details of other Isle of Man legislation on copyright and design rights, and the relevant Manx Government circulars issued by way of secondary legislation, see [1994] 1 *EIPR*, p. iv.

As far as the United Kingdom itself is concerned, the relevant sections of the U.K. 1988 Act have been applied, under the provisions of section 159, to residents, etc., of the Isle of Man (Copyright (Application to the Isle of Man) Order 1992, (S.I. 1992 No. 1313), text in *Copyright* 1992, November).

Rental

The provisions as regards the rental right are the same as under the U.K. 1988 Act: see paragraph 20.31.

Convention membership

According to the information supplied by the Intellectual Property Policy Department of the United Kingdom Patent Office, the Universal Copyright Convention (1971 text) and the Phonograms Convention have been extended to the Isle of Man (on September 6, 1972, and December 4, 1974, respectively); the Berne Convention (Paris text 1971), the Rome Convention, the WIPO Convention and the European Agreement concerning Programme Exchanges by means of Television Films have not, as at January 1, 1994, been extended to the Isle of Man.

U (P), P.

Remedies and penalties

The civil remedies under the 1991 Act are similar to those under the U.K. 1988 Act (ss.96–102). As passed in 1991, the Isle of Man Act provides in section 106 a range of penalties similar to those under the U.K. 1988 Act (*i.e.* imprisonment or fine, or both), though the levels are different.

[January 1994]

Italy

Performers' rights

Law No. 93 of February 5, 1992 contains provisions regulating the administration of the remuneration due to performers for the broadcasting or public performance of sound recordings, arising under art. 73 of the 1941 Law: the administering body is the Performers Mutual Institute (IMAIE).

Cartoon films

As to protection of cartoon films under Italian law see Fabiani, M., "La durata di protezione dei cartoni animati di Walt Disney" *Il Diritto di Autore* 1992, 575.

Blank tape payment

A system of payments on blank audio and video tapes and audio recording machine equipment has been instituted in Italy: see paragraph 20.28.

Rental

See paragraph 20.31.

E.C. Directives

It is anticipated that legislation will be introduced to implement the provisions of E.C. Directives 92/100 (rental and lending rights, and related rights), 93/83 (satellite broadcasting and cable retransmission), and 93/98 (term of protection), in so far as existing Italian law needs to be revised in this connection (*cf.* para. 7.51, and see para. 20.20).

[January 1994]

Jamaica

33.10 The main text entry is replaced by the following, in consequence of the adoption of a new copyright law in 1993.

— Copyright Act 1993

Literary, dramatic, musical and artistic works: Level I(m) protection by copyright for author (50 years p.m.a.).

Performances: Level IV protection for performances by performer's right (50 years).

Sound recordings: Level I protection by copyright for producer (50 years).

Films: Level I protection by copyright for producer (50 years).

Broadcasts and cable programmes: Protected under Copyright Act 1993.

General comments

The Jamaica Copyright Act 1993 repeals the previous copyright legislation and adopts many of the provisions of the U.K. Copyright, Designs and Patents Act 1988, with variations on a number of points. It establishes a high standard of protection as regards literary, etc., works, sound recordings and films.

Cabling

Broadcasting by wireless telegraphy and cabling are treated as separate acts (s.2(1)), owners of copyright being granted exclusive rights in regard to each type of use (s.9(d)).

Performers' rights

Performers have rights concerning the making of recordings of their performances, or the live broadcasting of cabling of protected performances (s.108).

However, performers have no specific right under the Act to authorise or receive remuneration for the broadcasting, cabling or public performance of their legitimately recorded performances (though they do have rights concerning use of illicit recordings: s.109).

Sound recordings

The provisions regarding the protection of sound recordings are similar to those of the U.K. 1988 Act (*cf.* main text para. 45.70), without the "licence of right" sections, 135A–135G.

Films

The provisions regarding protection of films are similar to those of the U.K. 1988 Act (see main text para. 45.70). As under the U.K. 1988 Act, the director of a protected film has moral rights (ss.14,15).

Computer programs

Computer programs are protected as literary works (ss.2(1), 6(1)).

Persons having recording rights

Persons having recording rights regarding performances enjoy protection against unauthorised recording, etc., of the performances concerned (ss.112–114). *Quaere,* whether, according to the wording of section 112, the contract with the performer must be exclusive.

Rental

Owners of copyright in sound recordings, films and computer programs are granted rental rights: see paragraph 20.31.

Convention membership

Jamaica has acceded to the Berne Convention (Paris text 1971), with a declaration as to Articles II and III of the Appendix, with effect from January 1, 1994: see *Copyright* 1993, 243.

Jamaica has acceded to the Rome Convention with, effect from January 27, 1994: see *Copyright* 1994, 23.

Jamaica has acceded to the Phonograms Convention, with effect from January 11, 1994: see *Copyright* 1993, 254.

B (P), R, P, W.

Remedies and penalties

There are extensive provisions as to civil remedies for infringement of copyright and moral rights (ss.29–43). Criminal penalties for offences under the Act include (according to the offence):

(a) on summary conviction: fine up to $100,000 or imprisonment up to two years, or both;
(b) on Circuit Court conviction: fine (unlimited) or imprisonment up to five years, or both.

See section 46.

[January 1994]

Japan

33.20 — Amending Law No. 106 of December 16, 1992 (*Copyright* 1993, October) (blank tape payments)

Private copying compensation

A system of payment for compensation in respect of sound or visual recording on a digital recording medium for private use is established by the Law of December 16, 1992: see para. 20.28.

Duration of protection

Correction. The period of protection for performances (as well as for phonograms) was extended to 50 years by the 1991 amending Law (art. 4, amending art. 101 of the 1970 Law), with effect from January 1, 1992.

Main text reference to 1991 Law

The reference to the 1991 amending Law (see main text) should read as follows:

— Law (Amendments) No. 63 of May 2, 1991 (*Copyright* 1992, January) (duration and rental)

The date of the Law is May 2, 1991, not April 24, 1991.

Remedies and penalties

The 1991 amending Law provides penalties of up to one year's imprisonment or fine of up to 300,000 yen for unauthorised making, possession or distribution of commercial phonograms (art. 121*bis*).

[January 1994]

Jordan

— Law on author's right, No. 22 of 1992

Literary, dramatic, musical and artistic works: Level I(m) protection by author's right (30 years p.m.a.).

Performances: Level I(m) protection for performers (as authors) (30 years p.m.a.).

Cinematograph works: Level I(m) protection by author's right (30 years p.m.a.).

General comments

The 1992 Law repeals the Ottoman Law of May 8, 1912. While the 1992 Law provides extensive protection for authors and performers, it falls short of, or does not incorporate, the standards required by the Berne, Rome and Phonograms Conventions, *e.g.*:

(1) the general term of protection for works is 30 years p.m.a., not 50 years, as required by the Berne Convention;
(2) there is no protection under the Law for phonogram producers or broadcasting organisations, as required by the Rome Convention.

On the other hand:

(1) the duration of protection would satisfy the requirements of the U.C.C. (minimum 25 years p.m.a.);
(2) extensive moral rights are granted to authors (including those of attribution, divulgation, amendment, integrity and retraction).

As far as foreign works are concerned, the International Conventions and the principle of reciprocity apply (art. 53).

It could be anticipated that the new Jordanian Law is a stage in the progress towards the granting of rights in conformity to the above-mentioned International Conventions, and it certainly marks an advance on the previous situation.

Moral rights

The author's moral rights include those of attribution, divulgation, prevention of distortion and, subject to conditions including compensation, withdrawal (art. 8).

Performers' rights

A notable feature of the 1992 Law is that, without prejudice to the rights of the author of the original work, the performer (performing in public) enjoys protection and is deemed to be an author (art. 5). This would appear to invest the performer with all the rights granted to authors of literary, dramatic, musical, etc., works. In other laws, the tendency has been to grant the performer a separate right, of a nature different from the right of a "traditional" author in the literary, etc, work: *cf.* main text paragraph 7B.02.

Broadcasting

A compulsory licence is given to broadcast works performed publicly in theatres, etc., subject to compensation (art. 23).

Cinematographic works

The authors of the screenplay, adaptation, dialogue and specially composed music and the director are the co-authors of the cinematographic work. The producer is the agent of the co-authors for the purpose of exploitation of the work (art. 37).

Deposit

The deposit formalities must be completed before action for infringement can be taken (art. 45).

Remedies and penalties

As well as civil remedies (arts. 46–50) criminal penalties for sale, etc., of infringing copies are fixed at imprisonment for not less than three months, plus fine of not less than 500 dinars, or more than 1,000 dinars, or either such imprisonment or fine. Repetition of an offence can result in the maximum term of custodial punishment, plus closure of establishment.

[January 1994]

Kazakhstan (New entry)

Pending notice of new legislation affecting the situation (see para. 21.01, Republics which formed part of the U.S.S.R. on May 31, 1991) it is assumed that protection continues as it was understood to be under the law applying before May 31, 1991, and the following synopsis is on that basis.

Literary, dramatic, musical and artistic works: Level I(m) protection by author's right (25 years p.m.a.).

Audiovisual works: Level I(m) protection by author's right (exploitation rights to producer) (25 years p.m.a.).

Convention membership

Kazakhstan has confirmed its membership of the Universal Copyright Convention (Geneva text 1952) by declaration of July 16, 1992: see *UNESCO Cop. Bull.* 1993, XXVII/1/5.

Kazakhstan has confirmed its membership of the WIPO Convention: see *Copyright* 1993, 49.

U (G), W.

[January 1994]

Kenya

Convention membership

Kenya has acceded to the Berne Convention (Paris text 1971), with effect from June 11, 1993: see *Copyright* 1993, 61.

Add to the Convention membership abbreviations: B (P).

[January 1994]

Kirghizia (New entry)

33.75 Pending notice of new legislation affecting the situation (see para. 21.01, Republics which formed part of the U.S.S.R. on May 31, 1991) it is assumed that protection continues as it was understood to be under the law applying before May 31, 1991, and the following synopsis is on that basis.

Literary, dramatic, musical and artistic works: Level I(m) protection by author's right (25 years p.m.a.).

Audiovisual works: Level I(m) protection by author's right (exploitation rights to producer) (25 years p.m.a.).

Convention membership

Clarification of application of the U.C.C. and WIPO Convention membership is awaited.

[January 1994]

Latvia (New entry)

34.35 — Law on Author's Right and Neighbouring Rights, of May 11, 1993

Literary, dramatic, musical and artistic works: Level I(m) protection by author's right (50 years p.m.a.).

Performances: Level I(m) protection by performer's right (50 years).

Sound recordings: Level IIx protection by producer's right (50 years).

Audiovisual works: Level I(m) protection by author's right (50 years).

Broadcasts: Protected by the Law of May 11, 1993.

General comments

Cabling

Making the work available to the public by cable, wire or other analogous means is one of the activities specifically covered by the exclusive economic rights of the author (art. 14(7)).

Audiovisual works

The director, the author of the scenario, the author of the specially composed musical work, the cameraman and the producer are (according to the translation confirmed by the Latvian Government) recognised as authors of the audiovisual work (art. 11(1)). The contributing authors retain their rights in their respective works, unless otherwise agreed by contract (art. 11(2)). However, article 12 provides that the moral and economic rights in works created under an employment contract belong to the employer, so where this applies, the producer will own the rights of the contributing authors.

The Latvian Law is unusual in specifying the producer as one of the authors of the audiovisual work. The specification of the cameraman as an author is also unusual, though not without precedent as far as recognition of status is concerned (*cf.* German law, main text para. 30.20).

Producer's rights

In the available translation, public performance (as distinct from broadcasting and cabling) is not specifically included among the producer's rights. Furthermore, it is not entirely clear from the translation whether the producer's right in respect of the broadcasting and cabling of commercially published sound recordings is exclusive, or for equitable remuneration. Pending clarification of this point, Level IIx is ascribed.

Rental

Rental rights are instituted for authors, performers and sound recording producers: see paragraph 20.31.

Convention membership

Latvia has acceded to the WIPO Convention, with effect from January 21, 1993 (see *Copyright* 1992, 235).
Clarification of application of the U.C.C. is awaited.

W.

Remedies and penalties

The Law provides for civil and criminal proceedings, together with remedies by way of forfeiture, etc. (arts. 54–57).

[January 1994]

Lithuania (New entry)

34.90 Pending notice of new legislation affecting the situation (see para. 21.01, Republics which formed part of the U.S.S.R. on May 31, 1991) it is assumed that protection continues as it was understood to be under the law applying before May 31, 1991, and the following synopsis is on that basis. For the current situation, see Pisuke, H. and Ilja M.-E., "Copyright developments in the Baltic States" *Copyright World* 1993, July/August, 30.

Literary, dramatic, musical and artistic works: Level I(m) protection by author's right (25 years p.m.a.).

Audiovisual works Level I(m) protection by author's right (exploitation rights to producer) (25 years p.m.a.).

Convention membership

Lithuania has acceded to the WIPO Convention, with effect from April 30, 1992: see *Copyright* 1992, 65.
Clarification of application of the U.C.C. is awaited.

W.

[January 1994]

Luxembourg

E.C. Directives

35.00 It is anticipated that legislation will be introduced to implement the provisions of E.C. Directives 92/100 (rental and lending rights, and related rights), 93/83 (satellite broadcasting and cable retransmission), and 93/98 (term of protection), in so far as existing Luxembourg law needs to be revised in this connection (*cf.* para. 7.51 and see para. 20.20).

[January 1994]

Macedonia (New Entry)

35.20 Pending notice of new legislation affecting the situation (see para. 21.01, Former Yugoslavia) it is assumed that protection continues as outlined in main text paragraph 47.60, Yugoslavia, and the following synopsis is on that basis.

Literary, dramatic, musical and artistic works: Level I(m) protection by author's rights (50 years p.m.a.).

Performances: Level IIx(m) protection by performer's right (20 years).

Cinematographic works: Level I(m) protection by author's right (50 years p.m.a.) (last surviving author).

Convention membership

Macedonia has confirmed its succession to membership of the Berne Convention (Paris text 1971): see *Copyright* 1993, 177.
 Macedonia has confirmed its succession to membership of the WIPO Convention: see *Copyright* 1993, 177.
 Clarification of application of the U.C.C. is awaited.

B(P), W.

[January 1994]

Malta

Act No. 20 of 1992 amends section 2(1) of the Copyright Act 1967 by adding "computer software" to the list of works included in the term "literary work".
 It is also reported that the provisions regarding penalties for copyright infringement were amended in 1992.

[January 1994]

Mexico

Remedies and penalties

Under the Decree of July 9, 1991, penalties for infringement of rights may (according to the offence) reach five years imprisonment, or five hundred times the daily minimum wage.

[January 1994]

Moldova   (New entry: formerly listed as Moldovia)

Pending notice of new legislation affecting the situation (see para. 21.01 Republics which formed part of the U.S.S.R on May 31, 1991) it is assumed that protection continues as it was understood to be under the law applying before May 31, 1991, and the following synopsis is on that basis.

Literary, dramatic, musical and artistic works: Level I(m) protection by author's right (25 years p.m.a.).

Audiovisual works: Level I(m) protection by author's right (exploitation rights to producer) (25 years p.m.a.).

Convention membership

Moldova has confirmed its membership of the WIPO Convention: see *Copyright* 1993, 119. Clarification of application of U.C.C. membership is awaited.

W.

[January 1994]

Montenegro (New entry)

37.00 Pending notice of new legislation affecting the situation (see para. 21.01, Former Yugoslavia) it is assumed that protection continues as outlined in main text paragraph 47.60, Yugoslavia, and the following synopsis is on that basis.

Literary, dramatic, musical and artistic works: Level I(m) protection by author's right (50 years p.m.a.).

Performances: Level IIx(m) protection by performer's right (20 years).

Cinematographic works: Level I(m) protection by author's right (50 years p.m.a.) (last surviving author).

Convention membership

Clarification of the application of the Berne Convention and the U.C.C., and of WIPO membership is awaited.

[January 1994]

Namibia (New entry)

37.40 It is understood that new copyright legislation has been enacted in Namibia. As to the situation before the coming into force of the new legislation, the Minister of Information and Broadcasting has confirmed that copyright protection in Namibia was on the basis of the South African Copyright Act 1965 (though without the amendments of 1967, 1972, 1975 and 1978): the following synopsis is on that basis, and will need to be amended in the light of the terms of the new legislation.

Literary, dramatic, musical and artistic works: Level I protection by copyright for author (50 years p.m.a.).

Sound recordings: Level IV protection by copyright for maker (50 years).

Cinematograph films: Level I protection by copyright for maker (50 years).

Broadcasts: Protected as under South African Copyright Act 1965.

General comments

In general, the South African Copyright Act 1965 follows the main provisions of the U.K. Copyright Act 1956. However, the protection for sound recordings is, under the 1965 Act, limited to the reproduction right. Namibia has thus, at present, taken over the restricted protection in this area as afforded by the South African legislation.

The South African Performers Protection Act 1967 does not apply in Namibia.

Convention membership

Namibia has acceded to the Berne Convention (Paris text 1971), with effect from December 24, 1993: see *Copyright* 1993, 243.

B(P), W.

[January 1994]

Netherlands

— Law of March 18, 1993 (neighbouring rights, and amendment of Author's Right Law 1912 (cabling, film exploitation, etc.))

Performances: Level Ix(m) protection by neighbouring right for performer (50 years).

Phonograms: Level Ix protection by neighbouring right for producer (50 years).

General comments

Recognition of neighbouring rights

The Law of March 18, 1993 establishes neighbouring rights in Dutch law, as indicated above.

Cabling

The general term "transmission" (*uitzenden*) covers both wireless broadcasting and cabling (art. 1.). Performers and phonogram producers have exclusive rights concerning transmission, or other form of public communication (subject to art. 7, see below).

Remuneration rights of performers and producers

Performers and phonogram producers have remuneration rights where commercially published phonograms are used for transmission (broadcasting or cabling) or other public use, the principle of Article 12 of the Rome Convention thus being recognised in Dutch law (art. 7) (*cf.* para. 7B.07). This evolution is of particular interest in view of the position of the Netherlands at the Rome Conference 1961: *cf.* paragraph 7A.10.

Private copying

Performers, phonogram producers and broadcasting organisations are entitled to share in the remuneration arising under article 16(c)-(g) of the Author's Right Law 1912, as amended: see paragraph 20.28.

E.C. Directives

It is anticipated that legislation will be introduced to implement the provisions of E.C. Directives 92/100 (rental and lending rights, and related rights), 93/83 (satellite broadcasting and cable retransmission), and 93/98 (term of protection), in so far as existing Dutch law needs to be revised in this connection (*cf.* para. 7.51, and see para. 20.20).

Convention membership

The Netherlands has acceded to the Rome Convention, with reservations, with effect from October 7, 1993: see *Copyright* 1993, 253.

The Netherlands has acceded to the Phonograms Convention, with effect from October 12, 1993: see *Copyright* 1993, 120.

Add to the Convention membership abbreviations:
Rr, P.

Remedies and penalties

In addition to civil remedies (including damages or account of profits) (art. 16) and seizure and delivery up provisions (art. 17), criminal sanctions for infringement of neighbouring rights may, according to the type of offence, and the occupation of the convicted person, involve imprisonment for up to four years or fine of the fifth category (at present Hfl. 100,000) (arts. 21–31). Remedies available under the general civil wrong provisions of the Civil Code 1989 (art. 6(12)) remain applicable.

[The author is grateful to Freyke Bus for comments on the above synopsis.]
[January 1994]

Niger

It is reported that Law 93/93 establishes protection for author's right, neighbouring rights and expressions of folklore. 38.40
[January 1994]

Nigeria

— Copyright (Amendment) Decree 1992 (Decree No. 98 of December 28, 1992) 38.50

The 1992 Decree effects a number of amendments to the Copyright Decree 1988, including the following.

Author of sound recording

Section 39 is amended to provide that in the case of a sound recording, "author" means the person by whom the arrangements for the making of the sound recording were made, but in the case of a sound recording of a musical work, the author is the artist in whose name the recording was made, unless in either case the parties contractually agree otherwise.

Private copying

A levy is imposed on any material used or capable of being used to infringe copyright in a work: the beneficiaries are not at present specified: see paragraph 20.28.

Performers' rights

See Sodipo B., "Nigeria accedes to the Rome Convention: is Rome satisfactory for Nigerian performers?" [1994] *Ent. L.R.* 20.

Convention membership

Nigeria has acceded to the Berne Convention (Paris text 1971), with effect from September 14, 1993: see *Copyright* 1993, 119.

Nigeria has acceded to the Rome Convention, with reservations, with effect from October 29, 1993: see *Copyright* 1993, 253.

Add to the Convention membership abbreviations:
B(P), Rr.

[The author is grateful to Bankole Sodipo for provision of material, and for comments on the above synopsis.]

[January 1994]

Norway

38.90 It is reported that article 54 of the Law of May 12, 1961 was amended to provide a new offence of importing, without the producer's consent, copies of a sound recording for commercial purposes, where copies of such recording are available in Norway with the producer's consent. This remedy is apparently intended to cover "parallel importation", and is in addition to those already provided regarding importation.

[January 1994]

Poland

40.30 It is reported that Poland has adopted a new Author's Right and Neighbouring Rights Law, signed by the President on February 4, 1994. Among other provisions, the Law increases the basic term of protection. See Preface.

Sound recordings

For a general summary of the previous protection of sound recordings in Poland, see Dietz, A. in [1993] *Ent. L.R.* 99.

[February 1994]

Portugal

40.40 A translation of the Code on Author's Right and Related Rights 1985, as amended by Law 114/91 of September 3, 1991, is published in *Copyright* 1992, September/October.

SYNOPSIS OF LAWS, CHARTS, ETC.   41.00

E.C. Directives

It is anticipated that legislation will be introduced to implement the provisions of E.C. Directives 92/100 (rental and lending rights, and related rights), 93/83 (satellite broadcasting and cable retransmission), and 93/98 (term of protection), in so far as existing Portuguese law needs to be revised in this connection (*cf.* para. 7.51, and see para. 20.20).

[January 1994]

Romania

Sound recordings

For a general summary of the protection of sound recordings in Romania, see Dietz, A. in [1993] *Ent. L.R.* 99.   41.00

[January 1994]

Russian Federation   (New entry)

— Law of July 9, 1993, on Author's Right and Neighbouring Rights (*Copyright*   41.10
   1994, January)
— Resolution of the Supreme Soviet of the Russian Federation of July 9, 1993 (on entry into force of the Law on Author's Right and Neighbouring Rights)

See also Law of September 23, 1992, on the Legal Protection of Computer Programs and Databases, and Law of September 23, 1992, on the Legal Protection of Semiconductor Topographies.

The Fundamentals of the Civil Legislation of the U.S.S.R. and Union Republics (Title IV) of May 31, 1991 were published in *Copyright* 1993, May, together with the Resolution of the Supreme Soviet of the Russian Federation on the Regulation of Civil Legal Relations during the Implementation of the Economic Reform, dated July 14, 1992. Title IV was declared void on the territory of the Russian Federation from the coming into force of the Law of July 9, 1993 (Resolution of July 9, 1993, paragraph 10).

The references in the following synopsis are to the Law of July 9, 1993, the new author's right and neighbouring rights law of the Russian Federation. The Law has entered into force: the transitional and implementation provisions are incorporated in the above-mentioned Resolution of July 9, 1993.

The translation of the Law published in *Copyright* uses the term "copyright", but the literal translation of the Russian term used in the Law is "author's right" (*avtorskoye pravo*).

Literary, dramatic, musical and artistic works: Level I(m) protection by author's right (50 years p.m.a.).

Performances: Level Ix(m) protection by neighbouring right for performer (50 years)

Phonograms: Level Ix protection by neighbouring right for producer (50 years)

Audiovisual works: Level I(m) protection by author's right (exploitation rights to producer) (50 years p.m.a. (last surviving author)).

Broadcasting organisations: Protected under the Law of July 9, 1993.

General comments

The Russian Federation's Law of July 9, 1993 marks an important advance in the level of protection granted, by comparison to the situation obtaining under the U.S.S.R. Fundamentals of Civil Legislation 1961, notably in abolishing the previous compulsory licences, recognising unfettered exclusive rights to the author, extending the general period of protection to 50 years p.m.a., instituting a private copying remuneration system, recognising the rental right, and recognising the neighbouring rights of performers, phonogram producers and broadcasting organisations.

As regards author's rights the protection appears to be basically in conformity with the requirements of the Berne Convention (Paris text 1971). Rights come into existence without formalities (art. 9).

As regards neighbouring rights, the 1993 Law grants greater protection than that required under the Rome Convention 1961, in several respects, including granting of moral-type rights to performers, granting performers rental rights, retention by performers of certain rights on the occasion of audiovisual recordings (art. 37(6), *cf.* Rome Convention, Art. 19) and granting a basic period of 50 years' protection (art. 43(1), the "moral" rights of attribution and integrity being unlimited in time). Phonogram producers are granted exclusive rights of reproduction, adaptation, distribution and importation (art. 38), and the right to equitable remuneration for public performance, broadcasting and cabling of phonograms (art. 39): the basic term is 50 years, art. 43(2).

Cable distribution organisations, as well as broadcasting organisations, are granted rights protecting their transmissions (arts. 40 and 41): the basic term is 50 years, art. 43(3)(4).

In sum, the Russian Federation now has, it is thought, an author's right and related rights law as advanced in concept, and in dealing with technological developments, as any comparable legislation. In the field of duration of rights, the Russian Federation, like many other countries, will have to increase the term of 50 years p.m.a., if it is to harmonise with the European Union standard: see paragraph 7.51C.

Author's rights

The author's rights include moral rights (covering attribution, disclosure, integrity of work and reputation and (subject to compensation) retraction) (art. 15). The rights of attribution and integrity continue indefinitely (art. 27(1)), irrespective of transfer of the economic rights (art. 15(3)).

The author's rights also include exclusive economic rights of exploitation, which are of a wide compass and include reproduction, distribution (including rental), importation (including importation (for distribution) of legitimately made copies), public performance, broadcasting, cabling, translation, and adaptation (art. 16). There is also a *droit de suite* for fine art authors (art. 17).

Computer programs and databases

Computer programs and databases are specifically protected (art. 7(2)(3)), and there are provisions concerning decompilation, etc. (art. 25).

Reproduction

The 1993 Law distinguishes between "reproduction of a work" (making one or more copies of a work) and "recording" (fixing of sounds or images or both in a material form) (art. 4). This classification is in harmony with the distinction made in main text paragraph 2.36, between a reproduction as a copy, and a recording pattern resulting from the fixation of sounds or images.

Storage of a work in a computer memory constitutes reproduction (art. 4).

Broadcasting and cabling

Broadcasting refers to communication to the public by means of transmission by radio and television, excluding cabling. Broadcasting includes satellite transmissions which may communicate works, etc., to the public, irrespective of actual reception (art. 4).

The act of communication to the public by cable is separate from that of broadcasting (art. 4).

Audiovisual works

The director, the author of the scenario and the author of the specially created musical work are recognised as authors of the audiovisual work (art. 13(1)). On conclusion of the contract for the making of the audiovisual work, the producer acquires the exploitation rights, unless otherwise provided in the contract (art. 13(2)).

Works made for hire

Author's right in works created by an employee in the execution of his duty belongs to the employee (with exceptions regarding encyclopedias, etc.): the employer has exclusive rights to use the work, unless the contract otherwise provides (art. 14).

Performers' rights

Performers' rights include the "moral" rights of attribution and integrity, and an exclusive exploitation right, including exclusive rights of broadcasting, cabling and fixation of live performances, reproduction of fixations (with limitations similar to those provided by the Rome Convention), broadcasting or cabling of non-commercial recordings and rental (art. 37(1)-(3)). In addition, performers have a remuneration right regarding performance, etc., of phonograms (see below).

The conclusion of the contract between the performer and the producer of an audiovisual work entails transfer of the exploitation rights (but not right of separate use of sounds or images in the work) (art. 37(6)).

Phonogram producers' rights

Phonogram producers have an exclusive right to exploitation of the phonogram in any form, and right to receive remuneration for every type of use of the phonogram (art. 38(1)). Producers' exclusive rights include those of reproduction, adaptation or other transformation, distribution (including rental) and importation (including importation of legitimately made copies, subject to exhaustion rule) (art. 38(2)). In addition, phonogram producers have a remuneration right regarding performance, etc., of phonograms (see below).

Remuneration for public performance, broadcasting or cabling of phonograms

Remuneration is payable for the public performance, broadcasting or cabling to the public of commercially published phonograms, the principle of Article 12 of the Rome Convention thus being recognised (art. 39(1)). In the absence of agreement, the remuneration is to be shared equally between performers and producers (art. 39(2)). The remuneration is administered collectively (art. 39(2)-(4)).

Private copying

A system of remuneration for authors, performers and phonogram producers is instituted in respect of private copying: see paragraph 20.28.

Rental

Rental rights are granted to authors, performers and phonogram producers: see paragraph 20.31.

Convention membership

The provisions of International Conventions to which the Russian Federation is party prevail over the domestic law, where there is a conflict (art. 3).

The Russian Federation has confirmed its membership of the Universal Copyright Convention (Geneva text 1952) by note of December 26, 1991: see *UNESCO Cop. Bull.* 1993, XXVII/1/6. The U.C.C. (Paris text 1971) applies to the works of authors of the Russian Federation: see *UNESCO Cop. Bull.* 1993, XXVII/1/16.

The Russian Federation has confirmed its membership of the WIPO Convention and the Satellites Convention: see *Copyright* 1992, 28.

U(G), W. See also paragraph 20.12 (Satellites).

Remedies and penalties

Civil, criminal and administrative remedies are provided for infringement of author's right and neighbouring rights (art. 48). Remedies may include indemnity up to 50,000 times the statutory (monthly) minimum wage (art. 49(1)(5)). Fines may be imposed (art. 49(2)). There are extensive provisions concerning confiscation, seizure, etc., of infringing copies (arts. 49(4), 50).

[The author is grateful to Igor Pozhitkov for the supply of material, and to Ksenia Orlova for comments on this section.]

[January 1994]

St Lucia

Convention membership

St. Lucia has acceded to the WIPO Convention, with effect from August 21, 1993: see *Copyright* 1993, 83.

St. Lucia has acceded to the Berne Convention (Paris text 1971), with effect from August 24, 1993: see *Copyright* 1993, 83.

Insert the Convention membership abbreviations:
B(P), W.

[January 1994]

St. Vincent and the Grenadines

41.80 The main text entry is replaced by the following, in consequence of the adoption of a new copyright law in 1989.

— Copyright Act 1989 (Act No. 53 of December 27, 1989) (*Copyright* 1993, February)

Literary, dramatic, musical and artistic works: Level I(m) protection by copyright for author (50 years p.m.a.).

Performances: Level Ix protection by performer's right (20 years).

Phonograms: Level Ix protection by producer's right (20 years).

Cinematographic and others audiovisual works: Level I(m) protection by copyright for author (50 years).

Broadcasts: Protected under Copyright Act 1989.

General comments

Broadcasting and cabling

"Broadcast" (transmission by radio or television) and "communication by cable" are separately defined (s.2).

Cinematographic and other audiovisual works

The author of a work is its creator or maker (s.2).

The list of literary, artistic and scientific works protectible under the 1989 Act include cinematographic or other audiovisual works (s.3).

Cinematographic and other audiovisual works must be original to receive copyright protection (s.5(1)), but section 12(3) provides that when a work is created by an author in the course of employment or under a contract of services, the author's rights (both moral and economic) vest in the employer or commissioner. While the attribution of economic rights to the employer, and in some cases the commissioner, is a familiar concept (*cf.*, for example, the "work made for hire" provisions of the U.S. Copyright Act (see para. 45.90)), the attribution of moral rights to an employer or commissioner being a body corporate is not usual, in terms of the general system of attribution of moral rights, since these are generally related to the personality of the individual (*cf.* main text para. 4.68).

Performers' rights

Performers are granted the exclusive right to broadcast, communicate by cable, record and reproduce their performance (s.25(1)). In addition, performers have the right to share in the remuneration arising from the record performing right (see below).

Rights of phonogram producers

Phonogram producers are granted exclusive rights concerning reproduction, importation and distribution (including rental, see below) of phonograms (s.30). In addition, phonogram producers have the right to share in the remuneration arising from the record performing right (see below). Phonogram producers' rights are linked to production in St. Vincent and the Grenadines (s.30(1)(a), (5)).

Remuneration from record performing right

Where a phonogram which has been lawfully made locally is used for broadcasting or communication to the public, the user of the phonogram must pay remuneration to the phonogram producer and the performer concerned (s.33).

It is assumed that cabling is included within the ambit of section 33 by virtue of the use of the phrase "communication to the public" (*cf.* s.13(c)).

It will be noted that the period of protection for phonograms is reduced from the 50 year period available under the application of the U.K. Copyright 1956 Act to 20 years. It is thought that this is an unusual, perhaps unique, case where a country's new copyright legislation reduces the period of protection for phonograms, as compared with the level previously subsisting. Possibly it was desired to align the law with the Rome Convention, which provides a 20 year minimum period (Art. 14), but many Rome Convention countries (*e.g.* France, Germany, the U.K.) grant the 50 year period of protection for phonograms, and the majority of countries now adopt this standard (see main text para. 20.25, as amended by para. 20.25).

Rental

Phonogram producers are granted rental rights: see paragraph 20.31.

Convention membership

U(P).

[January 1994]

San Marino

42.00 The main text entry is replaced by the following, in consequence of the adoption of a new author's right law in San Marino.

— Law No. 8 of January 25, 1991 (author's and performer's rights)

Literary, dramatic, musical and artistic works: Level I(m) protection by author's right (50 years p.m.a.).

Performances: Level II x(m) protection, but only by performer's right of remuneration (duration not stated).

Sound recordings: Level I protection by author's right (50 years p.m.a.).

Audiovisual works: Level I(m) protection by author's right (exploitation rights to producer) (50 years).

General comments

The new San Marino Law is based on the "author's right" approach and provides a high level of protection for authors.

As far as neighbouring rights are concerned, however, the level of protection for performers is below that required by the Rome Convention, and broadcasting organisations are not protected at all under this Law. On the other hand, the San Marino Law (rightly, it is submitted; *c.f.* main text para. 6.15) recognises sound recordings as works of the same category as literary, dramatic, musical and artistic works, the criterion of originality being required in the case of all such works (art. 5).

The structure of protection of author's rights

The author is granted moral rights together with patrimonial rights, and the right to economic use deriving from such rights, as provided in the Law (art. 1). The moral rights are extensive, and include those of status (*qualità*), integrity, divulgation, attribution, etc. (arts. 27–31).

The author has the exclusive right of economic use of the work in every form and manner: this right includes, among others, the right to use the work in reproduction or divulgation (art. 32).

Divulgation of the work is constituted by any act that brings the work to the perception (*conoscenza*) of the public, in particular by representation or reproduction (art. 44).

Representation is constituted by communication of the work to the public by any means, and, in particular, by public performance, and transmitting a broadcast in a public place (art. 45).

A radio emission towards a satellite is a representation (art. 45).

In sum, the San Marino Law adopts the basic approach of the French system (which classifies the major economic rights as representation and reproduction (*cf.* main text para. 6.25)). However, the San Marino law breaks new ground in the Continental author's right laws by including original sound recordings in the categories of protected works. While the U.S. Copyright Act and certain other statutes adopt the same approach (see main text para. 7.29, Protection system B) it is believed that the San Marino Law is the first law in Western Europe to do so.

Cabling

While cabling is not specifically mentioned in the general reference to "communication to the public" in article 45, it is clear from the extensive provisions of articles 67 to 70 dealing, *inter alia*, with cabling, that such use is within the author's exclusive prerogative. Articles 67 and 68 are also interesting as containing provisions defining the ambit and types of cabling activities, and decoding.

Computer programs

Computer programs are protected as literary works (if original), but the protection period in only ten years (arts. 6(c) and 42).

Performers' rights

Performers of a dramatic, literary or musical work have the right to equitable remuneration, to be paid by the person making a sound or audiovisual recording, or a broadcast of the work (but not it appears, public performance: hence the attribution of Level IIx in para. 7B.21) (art. 93). Performers are granted the "moral" right of integrity (art. 94). The above-mentioned rights do not apply where performers have been specifically remunerated in respect of the production (art. 95).

Performers also have a right of attribution (art. 97), not affected by the provisions of article 95.

It would seem that the protection thus accorded to performers falls short of that required by the Rome Convention, in that, for instance, performers appear not to have the possibility of preventing unauthorised recording, broadcasting and communication to the public of their live performance (Rome Convention, Art. 7; see main text para. 7B.07).

Definition of sound recording

Article 10 defines sound recordings as reproductions and recordings of sounds which are "reproducible in sound form independently of the supports on which the recording or method of reproduction are effected". This may be a reflection of the attempt at the Paris Conference of the Berne Convention 1896 to distinguish between reproduction instruments which themselves incorporate the reproduction device (such as musical boxes), and those where the reproduction requires the addition of another object, such as a tape (see Ricketson, *The Berne Convention 1886–1986*, paragraph 8.13).

Rights of producers of sound recordings

Sound recordings, if original, are protected by author's right (art. 5(b)). However, the author is not defined: it would seem that those who have made creative contributions to the recording process could be regarded as its authors (*cf.* main text paras. 6.09–6.15).

Furthermore, accenting the concept of the primacy of the author, article 25 specifically provides that, as in the case of audiovisual works, the producer of the sound recording is not to be considered as the author of the work. Thus, the producer (defined as the individual or legal person who assumes the initiative and responsibility for the realisation of the work) will not, in respect of such activities, be regarded as an author. It is thought, however, that an individual acting as producer and at the same time bringing a creative contribution to the recording may be so regarded.

In the case of audiovisual works there are specific provisions regarding acquisition of rights by the producer (see below), but there are no such provisions in the case of sound recording producers. Consequently, sound recording producers will have to obtain the economic exploitation rights through contract with the contributing authors.

It is submitted that there should be no basic difference in the way sound and audiovisual productions are treated (see main text para. 8.08). The precedent is awaited where a Continental author's right law combines the features of the San Marino and French Laws, and recognises rights for the authors of the creative contributions to the sound recording (as in San Marino), and separate "neighbouring rights" for producers (as in France).

Rights of producers of audiovisual works

The authors of the audiovisual work are defined (subject to the provisions on co-authorship, art. 20) as the authors of the plot, the settings (*sceneggiatura*), the dialogues, the "original" music and the director, as well as the author of the pre-existing protected work (art. 23). Article 24 specifically provides that the producer of the audiovisual work is not considered an author of the work. However, article 62 provides that the audiovisual work production contract imports, in default of contractual provision to the contrary, the cession to the producer of the right of economic exploitation of the work.

Rental

While rental is not specifically mentioned as a category of "communication to the public" in article 45, it would seem that the wide terms of that article, and the reference to divulgation in article 44 (see above), bring rental within the ambit of the rights of authors. However, this is subject to confirmation.

Convention membership

W.

Remedies and penalties

Articles 112 to 120 contain general provisions regarding civil remedies and criminal sanctions.

[January 1994]

Saudi Arabia

It is reported that Regulations governing the Deposit of Copyright Applications were issued under Royal Decree No. M/26 of March 11, 1992: see *Copyright World* 1993, October, 9.

[January 1994]

Serbia (New entry)

Pending notice of new legislation affecting the situation (see para. 21.01, Former Yugoslavia) it is assumed that protection continues as outlined in main text paragraph 47.60, Yugoslavia, and the following synopsis is on that basis.

Literary, dramatic, musical and artistic works: Level I(m) protection by author's right (50 years p.m.a.).

Performances: Level IIx(m) protection by performer's right (20 years).

Cinematographic works: Level I(m) protection by author's right (50 years p.m.a.) (last surviving author).

Convention membership

Clarification of the application of the Berne Convention and the U.C.C., and of WIPO membership is awaited.

[January 1994]

Seychelles

42.40 The text of the Copyright Act 1982 (together with the text of the Copyright (Registration) Regulations 1984) is reproduced in *Copyright* 1992, November.

[January 1994]

Slovak Republic (New entry)

42.65 The main text for Czechoslovakia (para. 27.60) is replaced by the following, in relation to the Slovak Republic. The entry is on the basis that the Slovak Republic continues to apply the following legislation:

— Law No. 35 of March 25, 1965, as modified and amended by Law No. 89 of March 28, 1990, and Federal Law No. 468 of November 1, 1991 (Czech and Slovak Republics).

It is also assumed that the Slovak Republic has adopted a Decree similar to Decree No. 115/1991 of March 15, 1991 (Ministry of Culture, Czech Republic: see para. 27.70).

Literary, dramatic, musical and artistic works: Level I(m) protection by author's right (50 years p.m.a.).

Performances: Level Ix protection by performer's right (50 years).

Phonograms: Level I protection by producer's right (50 years).

Cinematographic works: Level I(m) protection by author's right exercised by producer (50 years).

Broadcasts: protected under Law of March 25, 1965.

General comments

There are a number of points remaining for clarification following the separation of the Czech Republic and the Slovak Republic into two separate States, as from January 1, 1993, and it may, in consequence, be necessary to amend this entry accordingly, when further details are obtained.

Broadcasting

Article 16 of the 1965 Law, which permitted broadcast transmission of works, subject to remuneration to the author, has been amended by the Federal Law of

November 1, 1991, removing the compulsory licence and providing that simultaneous, integral and unchanged cabling of broadcasts is considered part of the original broadcast.

Blank tape payment

The former system of payment on blank tape is retained: see paragraph 20.28.

Sound recordings

For a general summary of the protection of sound recordings in the Slovak Republic, see Dietz, A. in [1993] *Ent. L.R.* 99.

Rental

Authors, performers, phonogram producers and broadcasting organisations have the right to receive remuneration for the rental of recordings of their respective productions: see paragraph 20.31.

Convention membership

The Slovak Republic has confirmed its membership of the Berne Convention (Paris text 1971), the Rome Convention (with reservations), and the Phonograms Convention, with effect from January 1, 1993: see *Copyright* 1993, 18, 120.

The Slovak Republic has confirmed its membership of the U.C.C. (Geneva text 1952 and Paris text 1971), with effect from January 1, 1993: see *UNESCO Cop. Bull.* 1993, XXVII/2/3, 4.

The Slovak Republic has confirmed its membership of the Audiovisual Works Registration Treaty, with effect from January 1, 1993: see *Copyright* 1993, 18, and paragraph 7.49.

B(P), U(P), Rr, P, W. See also paragraph 7.49 (AWR Treaty).

[January 1994]

Slovenia (New entry)

Pending notice of new legislation affecting the situation (see para. 21.01, Former Yugoslavia) it is assumed that protection continues as outlined in main text paragraph 47.60, Yugoslavia, and the following synopsis is on that basis. It is reported that the amended Law of 1978 has been taken into the law of Slovenia by its Constitution: see Krneta, S. in *GRUR Int.* 1993, 717, in particular footnote 64.

Literary, dramatic, musical and artistic works: Level I(m) protection by author's right (50 years p.m.a.).

Performances: Level Ix(m) protection by performer's right (20 years).

Cinematographic works: Level I(m) protection by author's right (50 years p.m.a.) (last surviving author).

Convention membership

Slovenia has confirmed its membership of, *inter alia*, the WIPO Convention and Berne Convention (Paris text 1971): see *Copyright* 1992, 145.

Slovenia has confirmed its membership of the Universal Copyright Convention (Paris text 1971) by declaration of October 28, 1992: see *UNESCO Cop. Bull* 1993, XXVII/1/6, 16.

B(P), U(P), W. See also paragraph 20.12 (Satellites).

[January 1994]

South Africa

— Copyright Amendment Act 1992

It is reported that the Copyright Act 1978 has been amended by the Copyright Amendment Act 1992. The amendments deal, *inter alia*, with certain aspects of the protection of sound recordings, and remedies: see Dean, H. in [1992] *Ent. L.R.*, E-61.

Protection of sound recordings

On the situation regarding the protection of sound recordings in South Africa, see Dean, O.H. in *Copyright World* 1993, October, 18.

[January 1994]

Spain

— Law 20/1992 of July 7, 1992 (amending Law 22/1987)
— Decree No. 1434 of November 27, 1992 (private copying payments, etc.)

See also *Copyright* 1991, November (Orders concerning associations managing rights arising under the Law of November 11, 1987); *Copyright* 1992, July/August (Royal Decree 1584/1991 concerning general registry of intellectual property).

The amendments to Law 22/1987 effected by Law 20/1992 include the following:

(1) Article 25, establishing payment of remuneration in respect of private copying, is reworded, the general scheme being retained (see para. 20.28).
(2) Article 103, concerning the right of performers to receive half the producer's remuneration from the public communication of phonograms, is redrafted, and a provision giving performers the right to participate in the negotiations with users is added.
(3) The provisions of article 127 concerning precautionary measures are amended.

Further regulations concerning private copying payments, etc., are contained in Decree 1434/1992: see *Copyright World* 1992, February, 12.

E.C. Directives

It is anticipated that legislation will be introduced to implement the provisions of E.C. Directives 92/100 (rental and lending rights, and related rights), 93/83 (satellite broadcasting and cable retransmission), and 93/98 (term of protection), in so far as existing Spanish law needs to be revised in this connection (*cf.* para. 7.51, and see para. 20.20).

Convention membership

Spain's membership of the Rome Convention became effective on November 14, 1991: see *Copyright* 1991, 221, where the reservations made by Spain are also listed.

[January 1994]

Sweden

A translation of the Law of December 30, 1960, as last amended by the Law of June 20, 1991, is published in *Copyright* 1993, January.

See also Law No. 1685 of 1992 (computer programs and semiconductor chip protection).

Film works: exploitation

Article 39 of the 1960 Law does not, apparently, refer to the right in the film work itself, as distinct from the right to produce a film of a literary or artistic work. Note also that article 39 does not apply to musical works. There are provisions similar to article 39 in the laws of Denmark (1961 Law, art. 42), Finland (1961 Law, art. 39, *quaere* the position as to musical works) and Norway (1961 Law, art. 39).

[January 1994]

Switzerland

43.70 The main entry is replaced by the following, in consequence of the adoption of a new author's right law in 1992.

— Law of October 9, 1992 (author's right and neighbouring rights) (*Copyright* 1993, September)

Literary, dramatic, musical and artistic works: Level I(m) protection by author's right (70 years p.m.a.).

Performances: Level Ix protection by neighbouring right for performer (50 years).

Phonograms: Level Ix protection by neighbouring right for producer (50 years).

Audiovisual works: Level I(m) protection by author's right (70 years p.m.a.): see note below.

Cinegrams: Level Ix protection by neighbouring right for producer (50 years).

Broadcasts: Protected under the Law of October 9, 1992.

General comments

The 1992 Law represents a total revision and updating of the situation obtaining under the Law of December 7, 1922, with introduction of new rights in accordance with current legislative trends, *e.g.* private copying right, rental right (though only for authors).

Cabling

Cabling is specifically included in the author's transmission and retransmission rights, article 10(2)(d) apparently having reference to originated cabling, and article 10(2)(e) to retransmission of transmitted works, where the operator is not the original transmitting organisation (*cf.* Berne Convention, Paris text 1971, Arts. 11(1)(ii), 11*bis*(1)(ii)).

Performers' exclusive rights as regards live performance include originated cabling, and cabling by retransmission, where the operator is not the original transmitting organisation (art. 33(2)(b)).

Cabling is apparently within the ambit of the uses of sound and audiovisual recordings for which an equitable remuneration is payable to the performer, with share to the producer (see below).

Article 22(1) provides that the right to make transmitted works perceivable simultaneously and unchanged, or to retransmit such works in the framework of a further transmission of a transmitted programme can only be exercised through an approved administration society. Retransmission to limited audiences in certain circumstances is allowed (art. 22(2): *cf. Altdorf*, main text para. 7.25, n. 13, Switzerland). Article 22(1) does not apply to retransmission of programmes of subscription television, or of programmes not receivable in Switzerland (art. 22(3)).

Computer programs

Computer programs are classified as works within the ambit of author's right (art. 2(3)). The protection period (as an exception to the general rule of 70 years p.m.a.) is 50 years p.m.a. (art. 29(2)(a)).

Duration of protection of audiovisual works

The calculation of the duration of protection (70 years p.m.a.) of audiovisual works is solely by reference to the director (art. 30(3)).

Performers' rights

Performers are granted exclusive rights regarding the recording, transmission, public performance, etc., of their performances (art. 33), in addition to a remuneration right in respect of secondary use of phonograms and videograms (see below).

Rights of producers of phonograms and cinegrams

Producers of sound carriers (*Tonträgern*) and sound-image carriers (*Tonbildträgern*) (herein respectively called phonograms and cinegrams: see main text para. 3.08) are granted exclusive rights of multiplication and distribution of their respective recordings (art. 36), in addition to a right to share in the performer's remuneration for the secondary use of phonograms and cinegrams (see below).

Remuneration right for use of phonograms and cinegrams

Performers are granted a right of equitable remuneration for transmission, retransmission and public reception or performance of phonograms or cinegrams (art. 35(1)). Producers of phonograms or cinegrams which have been so used are entitled to an equitable share of the performer's remuneration (art. 35(2)). Remuneration claims can only be made through an approved administration society (art. 35(3)). Foreign performers may claim the remuneration when their respective countries grant a corresponding right to Swiss citizens (art. 35(4)).

The adoption of the 1992 Law brings to a positive conclusion the long-debated question of the recognition of record performing rights in Switzerland: see main text paragraph 7A.05, and note that Switzerland has now ratified the Rome Convention, accepting the principle of Article 12 (see below, and main text para. 7A.10).

Duration of phonogram protection: previous law

A phonogram protection period of 50 years (also extending to foreign recordings) under the law in force before the adoption of the Law of October 9, 1992, was confirmed in *Elvis Presley Records, GRUR Int.* 1993, 707 (Swiss Federal Court, August 18, 1993).

Private use

Article 20(3) establishes system of payment of remuneration to the author in respect of private use of published works: see paragraph 20.28.

Rental

Article 13(1) grants the author a right of remuneration for rental: see paragraph 20.31.

Collecting societies and tariffs

There are extensive provisions concerning the approval and supervision of collecting societies and the applicable tariffs (arts. 40–66).

Convention membership

Switzerland has ratified the Paris text 1971 of the Berne Convention, with effect from September 25, 1993: see *Copyright* 1993, 119.

Switzerland has ratified the Paris text 1971 of the U.C.C., with effect from September 21, 1993: see *UNESCO Cop. Bull.* 1993, XXVII/2/4.

Switzerland has acceded to the Rome Convention, with reservations, with effect from September 24, 1993: see *Copyright* 1993, 254.

Switzerland has ratified the Phonograms Convention, with effect from September 30, 1993: see *Copyright* 1993, 120.

Switzerland has acceded to the Satellites Convention, with effect from September 24, 1993: see *Copyright* 1993, 254.

B(P), U(P), Rr, P, W. See also paragraph 20.12 (Satellites).

SYNOPSIS OF LAWS, CHARTS, ETC. 43.90

Remedies and penalties

Extensive civil remedies (including injunction, confiscation and damages) are provided in articles 61–66. Penalties for infringement (depending on the offence) include imprisonment (maximum term not stated) and fine (in certain cases up to 100,000 sfr.).

[January 1994]

Tadjikistan (New entry)

Pending notice of new legislation affecting the situation (see para. 21.01, Republics which formed part of the U.S.S.R. on May 31, 1991) it is assumed that protection continues as it was understood to be under the law applying before May 31, 1991, and the following synopsis is on that basis. 43.90

Literary, dramatic, musical and artistic works: Level I(m) protection by author's right (25 years p.m.a.).

Audiovisual works: Level I(m) protection by author's right (exploitation rights to producer) (25 years p.m.a.).

Convention membership

Tadjikistan has confirmed its membership of the Universal Copyright Convention (Geneva text 1952) by declaration of August 11, 1992: see *UNESCO Cop. Bull.* 1993, XXVII/1/6.
   Clarification of WIPO Convention membership is awaited.

U(G).

[January 1994]

Taiwan

The main text entry is replaced by the following, in consequence of the promulgation of a new author's right law in 1992. 44.00

— Law of June 10, 1992 (complete revision of law on author's right) ("the Copyright Law")
— Amending Law of July 6, 1992 (art. 53)
— Amending Law of April 24, 1993 (arts. 87, 87*bis*)
— Implementation Rules of the Copyright Law, of May 14, 1928, as amended September 5, 1944, May 27, 1955, August 10, 1959, May 11, 1965, June 16, 1986, November 27, 1989, March 12, 1990, June 10, 1992

— Rules illustrating content of works listed in article 5(1) of the Copyright Law of June 10, 1992
— Rules concerning royalty rates for public interest activities, of June 10, 1992
— Regulations concerning application for approval of compulsory licence of translation rights, of June 10, 1992
— Regulations concerning application for approval of compulsory licence of musical works, of June 10, 1992
— Organic Charter of the Copyright Examination and Mediation Committee of the Ministry of the Interior, promulgated August 28, 1992
— Regulations concerning copyright dispute mediation, promulgated September 23, 1992
— Rules concerning article 87*bis* of the Copyright Law, of April 24, 1993.

A complete revision of the 1928 Law was effected by the Law of June 10, 1992. In August 1993 the Minister of the Interior issued a translation of the new Law headed "Copyright Law of the Republic of China" and including the texts of various associated Rules and Regulations. The following synopsis is on the basis of that document. The term "copyright" is here used subject to the ascertainment of the literal translation of the term used in the original Chinese text.

Literary, dramatic, musical and artistic works: Level I(m) protection for author (50 years p.m.a.).

Sound recordings: Level I(m) protection by author's right (50 years).

Audiovisual works: Level I(m) protection by author's right (50 years).

General comments

Sound recordings

It is interesting to note that, as in the original text of the 1928 Law, sound recordings continue to be classified as author's works, gaining protection as original productions (arts. 3(1) and 5(8): *cf.* main text para. 44.00, Sound recordings).

Computer programs

Computer programs are protected as author's works in the same category as other original productions (arts. 3(1) and 5(10)).

Employee and commissioned works

The employee or commissioned person is the author of the work; the employer or commissioner may acquire rights by contract (arts. 11, 12).

SYNOPSIS OF LAWS, CHARTS, ETC.

Duration

The economic rights in a sound recording or audiovisual work (or computer program) endure for 50 years from public release of the work: in the case of such works (and where the author is a juridical person) the term is 50 years from completion, if the work has not been publicly released within ten years after completion (arts. 33, 34).

Cabling

"Public broadcast" means the activity of communicating the contents of a work with sounds or images by wire or wireless diffusion systems or other devices to the general public, where the purpose is reception by the general public (art. 3(7)).

Rental

All classes of authors of protected works are specifically granted the rental right: see paragraph 20.31.

Registration

Works may be registered, and there are extensive Rules in this regard (arts. 74 and 75 of the Implementation Rules as amended to June 10, 1992).

Convention membership

[. . .]

Remedies and penalties

Articles 84 to 90 concern available civil remedies: articles 91 to 104 deal with penal sanctions, which may, according to the offence, reach seven years imprisonment plus fine of 450,000 New Taiwan dollars.

[January 1994]

Thailand

Note the provisions of section 8 of the 1978 Law, concerning the rights of employers: this may govern the position where the author of an audiovisual work is an employee.

[January 1994]

Togo

44.30 The main text entry is replaced by the following, in consequence of the adoption of a new author's right and neighbouring rights law in 1991.

— Law No. 91-12 of June 10, 1991, on author's right and neighbouring rights (*Copyright* 1992, February)

Literary, dramatic, musical and artistic works: Level I(m) protection by author's right (50 years p.m.a.).

Performances: Level Ix protection by performer's right (25 years).

Phonograms: Level Ix protection by producer's right (25 years).

Cinematographic works: Level I(m) protection by author's right for producer (50 years).

Broadcasts: Protected under the Law of June 10, 1991.

General comments

Cinematographic works

Article 9 provides that the producer is invested with the rights in the cinematographic work. Article 10 provides that the contracts made by the producer with the authors of the screenplay, adaptation and spoken text, and the director, constitute assignment to the producer of the right of exploitation, subject to contractual terms to the contrary.

The Togolese Law therefore treats the rights in the cinematographic work, as such, as belonging to the producer, and the producer also acquires exploitation rights on the conclusion of contracts with the contributing authors (except the authors of music). This solution may be compared with the French system, under which the contributing authors have rights in the cinematographic work, such rights (subject to the contract) passing to the producer, who has a separate right in relation to the "videogram": see main text paragraph 29.30.

Cabling

Communication of the work to the public by wire is specifically included in the author's exclusive economic right.

Computer programs

Computer programs are protected as intellectual works (art. 6(xiv)).

Performers' rights

Article 96 establishes performers' rights on the model of the Rome Convention, Article 7, and in addition there is a right of remuneration for phonogram use in broadcasting or public communication (see below).

Phonogram producers' rights

Phonogram producers' rights are those of reproduction, importation and distribution (art. 103), with right of remuneration for phonogram performance (see below).

Phonogram performing right

Article 106 provides that remuneration is payable for the broadcasting or public communication of commercially published phonograms (*cf.* Art. 12 of the Rome Convention). The remuneration is to be shared 50/50 between performers and producers.

Protection of phonograms depends on the producer's Togolese nationality or domicil, or fixation or first publication in Togo (art. 116). If the phonogram which is used for broadcasting or public communication is unprotected, the respective share is to be paid to a national fund for the assistance and training of Togolese performers (art. 106). This is an interesting example of the adoption of a system similar to the one proposed in main text paragraphs 8.02, 8.14, namely that use of "unconnected" material should involve payment into a Cultural Promotion Fund in the user country.

Duration

While the Togolese 1991 Law may be regarded as modern in recognising neighbouring rights, it is our of step with current legislative trends in that it provides only a 25 year term of protection for such rights.

Convention membership

B(P), W.

Remedies and penalties

Articles 112 to 114 deal with civil remedies and criminal penalties, which may, in the case of neighbouring rights, reach 2,000,000 francs plus three years imprisonment.

[January 1994]

Tunisia

44.80 It is reported in *Copyright World* 1993, October, 9, that the Tunisian Law (No. 66-12 of February 14, 1966) has been revised.
Further details are awaited.

[January 1994]

Turkmenistan (New entry)

45.00 Pending notice of new legislation affecting the situation (see para. 21.01, Republics which formed part of the U.S.S.R. on May 31, 1991) it is assumed that protection continues as it was understood to be under the law applying before May 31, 1991, and the following synopsis is on that basis.

Literary, dramatic, musical and artistic works: Level I(m) protection by author's right (25 years p.m.a.).

Audiovisual works: Level I(m) protection by author's right (exploitation rights to producer) (25 years p.m.a.).

Convention membership

Clarification of application of the U.C.C. and WIPO Convention membership is awaited.

[January 1994]

Ukraine (New entry)

45.35 Pending notice of new legislation affecting the situation (see para. 21.01, Republics which formed part of the U.S.S.R. on May 31, 1991) it is assumed that protection continues as it was understood to be under the law applying before May 31, 1991, and the following synopsis is on that basis. As to new law, see Preface.

Literary, dramatic, musical and artistic works: Level I(m) protection by author's right (25 years p.m.a.).

Audiovisual works: Level I(m) protection by author's right (exploitation rights to producer) (25 years p.m.a.).

Convention membership

Clarification of application of the U.C.C. is awaited.

W.

[January 1994]

Union of Soviet Socialist Republics

For a summary of the position in the Republics of the former U.S.S.R., see paragraph 21.01: see also the entries in the Synopsis of Laws under the names of the respective Republics.

[January 1994]

United Arab Emirates (New entry)

— Federal Law No. 40 of September 28, 1992

Literary, dramatic, musical and artistic works: Level I(m) protection by author's right (25 years p.m.a.) (see note below).

Cinematographic works: Level I(m) protection by author's right (exploitation rights to producer) (25 years).

General comments

The United Arab Emirates consist of the Emirates of Abu Dhabi, Ajman, Dubai, Fujeirah, Rasal Khaimah, Sharjah and Umm al Qaiwain.

While the 1992 Law marks the first publication of specific legislation in the field of author's right in the United Arab Emirates, the Law would need to be amended in a number of respects if current international standards are to be met, and it is understood that discussions are proceeding in this connection. In particular the period of protection is below that provided by the Berne Convention, and there is no protection for performers, producers of phonograms and broadcasting organisations.

On the other hand, the Law recognises certain moral rights, including the attribution right, but not specifying the integrity right. The distribution right is widely defined and would appear to cover cabling, and possibly rental.

Cinematographic works

Those individuals who are considered the authors of cinematographic works are listed in article 26 (authors of the script, dialogue, adapter, specially composed music, the director and the author of the pre-existing work). The producer is granted exploitation rights (art. 29).

Computer programs

Computer programs are listed among the categories of created intellectual works, protected under the Law.

Convention membership

W. [January 1994]

United Kingdom

45.70 For the text of the Copyright (Application to the Isle of Man) Order 1992 (S.I. 1992 No. 1313), see *Copyright* 1992, November, and, for comment, see paragraph 32.70. (See also *Copyright* 1991, December (Order: recording for archives). The Act was further amended by the Copyright (Computer Programs) Regulations 1992 (S.I. 1992 No. 3233).

General comments

(a) *Protection under the 1988 Act*

(i) *Introductory* For details of the moral rights provisions of the 1988 Act, see main text paragraph 4.70.

(iii) *Films* For a survey of the questions arising regarding the use of underlying works see Stone, R., "Copyright in the underlying works of motion picture films: solving distribution and exploitation difficulties through declaratory relief" [1993] *Ent. L.R.* 40.

(c) *Protection under the U.K. Copyright Act 1911*

(ii) *Records* The Canadian Federal Court of Appeal has overruled the *Canadian Admiral* case, and held that broadcasting of a work to private homes constitutes public performance of the work: see paragraph 25.30.

E.C. Directives

It is anticipated that legislation will be introduced to implement the provisions of E.C. Directives 92/100 (rental and lending rights, and related rights), 93/83 (satellite broadcasting and cable retransmission), and 93/98 (term of protection), in so far as the existing law needs to be revised in this connection (*cf.* para. 7.51, and see para. 20.20).

Additional notes

(1) *United Kingdom and other territories*

Isle of Man The Isle of Man has adopted a separate Copyright Act: see paragraph 32.70.

A. REMEDIES UNDER THE COPYRIGHT, DESIGNS AND PATENTS ACT 1988

I *Copyright*

Criminal proceedings

Certain offences under the 1988 Act are punishable by fines "not exceeding the statutory maximum" or "not exceeding level 5 on the standard scale". These fines are specified in the main text as having a current maximum of £2,000.

The statutory maximum as at October 3, 1991 was £2,000: it has been increased, as at January 1, 1994, to £5,000.

Level 5 on the standard scale as at October 31, 1991, was £2,000: the system for calculating the fine in relation to the standard scale has been amended by the Criminal Justice Act 1991, section 18: it is related to a system of units, which vary in value according to the particular case, and the resultant fine may reach a maximum of £5,000.

Consequently "current maximum £2,000" should be replaced by "current maximum £5,000" wherever these words and figures appear in this section.

See Archbold *Pleading, Evidence and Practice in Criminal Cases* (Sweet & Maxwell, 1993) paragraphs 5-437 to 5-459.

III *Performers' rights*

The current maximum has been increased. Consequently "current maximum £2,000" should be replaced by "current maximum £5,000" wherever these words and figures appear in this section: see under I Copyright above.

IV *Recording rights (exclusive contracts)*

The current maximum has been increased. Consequently "current maximum £2,000" should be replaced by "current maximum £5,000" wherever these words and figures appear in this section: see under I Copyright above.

Remedies and penalties

For a recent survey, see Harbottle, G., "Criminal remedies for copyright and performers' rights infringement under the Copyright, Designs and Patents Act 1988" [1994] *Ent. L.R.* 12.

[January 1994]

United States of America

— Copyright Act 1976 (PL94-553) as last amended by the Audio Home Recording Act 1992 (PL102-563) (*Copyright* 1993, November/December)

(The North American Free Trade Agreement Implementation Act 1993 (PL103-182) of December 8, 1993 is published in *Copyright* 1994, February, but is not summarised here.)

A consolidated version of the U.S. Copyright Act 1976, as amended by enactments up to and including the Audio Home Recording Act 1992, is published in *Copyright* 1993, November, together with a list of the amending Acts incorporated in the consolidation. For a summary of the copyright legislation in the 102nd Congress covering these Acts, see 40 *J. Copr. Soc'y* 1 (1993).

(c) *Motion pictures and other audiovisual works*

(v) *Sound tracks* As to the copyright status of music in sound tracks of motion pictures released prior to 1978, see Brylawski, E.F., "Motion picture soundtrack music; a gap or gaff in copyright protection" 40 *J. Copr. Soc'y* 333 (1993).

(d) *The distribution right*

(ii) *Parallel imports* The first sale doctrine was held no defence in relation to parallel imports in *BMG Music v. Perex* 952 F. 2d 318 (U.S.C.A. 9, 1991).
Held, the first sale doctrine (s.109(a)) does not provide a defence where the defendant imported allegedly infringing perfume boxes acquired outside the United States: *Parfums Givenchy Inc. v. C & C Beauty Sales Inc.* 29 USPQ 2d 1026 (C.D.Calif. 1993): *cf.* paragraph 4.45.

(e) *Public performance*

In *National Football League v. McBee and Bruno's Inc.* 792 F. 2d 726 (U.S.C.A. 8, 1986), the defendant took football game transmission signals while they passed from a satellite to a distribution station, from which (with additions) they were sent to subscribers' homes. Held, violation of rights of display and performance under section 106 of the U.S. Copyright Act.

It was held in *Columbia Pictures Ind. Inc. v. Professional Real Estate Investors Inc.* 944 F. 2d 1525, 19 USPQ 2d 1771 (U.S.C.A. 9, 1991, cert. granted, 112 S.Ct. 1557 (1992)) that renting of videocassettes for playing by hotel guests in their rooms did not involve public performance.

In *On Command Video Corp. v. Columbia Pictures Ind. Inc.* 777 F. Supp. 787, 21 USPQ 2d 1545 (N.D.Calif. 1991) it was held, where a video viewing system permitted electronic delivery of video tape programmes to hotel rooms, that such rooms were not public places, but the system violated the provisions of section 101 of the 1976 Act, concerning "transmission".

In *NBC v. Satellite Broadcast Networks Inc.* 940 F. 2d 1467, 19 USPQ 2d 1071 (U.S.C.A. 11, 1991), it was held that broadcasts taken off-air and rebroadcast to home subscribers constituted a cable system which fell within the licence system available under section 111 of the 1976 Act.

In *National Cable Television Assn. v. BMI* 772 F. Supp. 614, 20 USPQ 2d 1481 (D.D.C. 1991) it was held that a cable television programmer's transmission of protected music to a cable system operator constituted public performance of the transmitted music.

In *Prophet Music Inc. v. Shamla Oil Co. Inc.* 26 USPQ 2d 1554 (D.Minn. 1993), the defendants ran a "music-on-hold" system, by which customers of their service station could receive radio programmes transmitted over the line, when they called the station by telephone. Thus the music contained in radio broadcasts was further transmitted over telephone lines to the defendant's customers making incoming telephone calls. Held: infringement by unauthorised public performance of the music. The "single receiving apparatus" defence under section 110(5) of the Copyright Act did not apply, and the broadcasts received by the defendants were "further transmitted" to the public within the meaning of section 110(5)(B). The plaintiffs were entitled to $500 statutory damages for each infringement, plus a permanent injunction.

Possibly this case will be of relevance when considering transmission of protected material to subscribers accessing databases storing films and phonograms.

Unintentional broadcasting of copyright music held infringement: *Coleman v. ESPN Inc.* 20 USPQ 2d 1513 (S.N.Y. 1991).

The "single receiving apparatus" exemption

The District Court judgement in *Broadcast Music Inc. v. Claire's Boutiques Inc.* has been affirmed: 949 F. 2d 1482, 21 USPQ 2d 118 (U.S.C.A. 7, 1991, cert. denied, 112 S.Ct. 1995, 118 L.Ed. 2d 590, 60 USLW 3781). Similarly the decision in *Edison Bros. Stores Inc. v. Broadcast Music Inc.* has been affirmed: 954 F. 2d 1419, 21 USPQ 2d 1440 (U.S.C.A. 8, 1992, cert. denied, 112 S.Ct. 1942, 118 L.Ed. 2d 457, 60 USLW 3780).

(g) *Convention membership*

As to the question of protection of works which have fallen into the public domain, in the context of the United States accession to the Berne Convention, see Regnier, O., "Who framed Article 18? The protection of pre-1989 works in the U.S.A. under the Berne Convention" [1993] *EIPR* 400.

Additional notes

(2) *Private copying*

A system of payments on digital audio recording devices and media, with participation by authors, performers and record companies, has been instituted by the Audio Home Recording Act 1992: see paragraph 20.31.

Serial copying control

Incorporation of serial copying controls into digital audio recording devices and interfaces is made compulsory by the Audio Home Recording Act 1992, section 1002.

(3) *Infringement of computer program copyright*

For United States cases on infringement of computer program copyright, see paragraphs 4.25, 4A.26.

(4) *Main text listing of U.S. Acts*

Correction. In the main text list of additional measures: (a) the reference to the amending Act 1976 is *Copyright* 1977, 336; (b) the title in the last line is Architectural Works Copyright Protection Act 1990.

Remedies and penalties

Section 1009 of the 1976 Act, as amended, provides civil remedies for violation of the Audio Home Recording Act 1992, including provisions as to actual and statutory damages.

The amending Act of October 28, 1992 (PL102-561) introduces amendments concerning: (a) penalties for trafficking in counterfeit labels for phonorecords and copies of motion pictures or other audiovisual works (fine up to $250,000 or imprisonment up to five years, or both); and (b) penalties for criminal infringement of copyright (including, according to offence, imprisonment up to ten years, or fine, or both).

In *U.S. Sporting Products Inc. v. Johnny Stewart Game Calls Inc.* (U.S. Texas C.A. 1993, 1993 Tex. App Lexis 2675, summary in [1994] *Ent. L.R.* E-12), it was held that relief on the basis of misappropriation (a branch of the law of unfair competition) was available in respect of the unauthorised copying of a recording of animal sounds.

[February 1994]

Uruguay

Convention membership

Uruguay has joined the Universal Copyright Convention (Geneva text 1952, Paris text 1971) by accession of January 12, 1993: see *UNESCO Cop. Bull.* 1993, XXVII/1/7, 15.

Add to the Convention membership abbreviations:
U(P).

[January 1994]

Uzbekistan (New entry)

Pending notice of new legislation affecting the situation (see para. 21.01, Republics which formed part of the U.S.S.R. on May 31, 1991) it is assumed that protection continues as it was understood to be under the law applying before May 31, 1991, and the following synopsis is on that basis.

Literary, dramatic, musical and artistic works: Level I(m) protection by author's right (25 years p.m.a.).

Audiovisual works: Level I(m) protection by author's right (exploitation rights to producer) (25 years p.m.a.).

Convention membership

Uzbekistan has confirmed its membership of the WIPO convention: see *Copyright* 1993, 83. Clarification on application of the U.C.C. is awaited.

W.

[January 1994]

Venezuela

The main text entry is replaced by the following, in consequence of the adoption of a revised Law in 1993.

— Law of August 14, 1993, on author's right and related rights

Literary, dramatic, musical and artistic works: Level I(m) protection by author's right (60 years p.m.a.).

Performances: Level Ix(m) protection by related right for performer (60 years).

Phonograms: Level Ix protection by related right for producer (60 years).

Audiovisual works: Level I(m) protection by author's right (exploitation rights to producer) (60 years).

Broadcasts: Protected under Law of August 14, 1993.

General Comments

Cabling

Article 39 states that the exploitation rights of the author consist of the right of public communication and the right of reproduction. Public communication is comprised by any act through which a number of persons have access to the work, particularly broadcasting, and transmission to the public by cable.

Audiovisual works

In default of contrary proof, the authors of the audiovisual works are presumed to be the director, the authors of the plot or adaptation, the script or dialogue and the specially composed music, together with the author of the pre-existing work. The director is empowered to exercise the moral rights over the work, without prejudice to those of the co-authors in relation to their respective contributions, and those which may be exercised by the producer (art. 12). The producer can be a co-author if he brings a creative contribution to the work (art. 14). It is presumed, subject to express contrary stipulation, that the authors of the audiovisual work have ceded the exploitation rights to the producer (art. 15). The producer may, without prejudice to the author's rights, and subject to contrary stipulation, "exercise in his own name the moral rights over the audiovisual work, to the extent necessary to exploit it" (art. 15). This latter provision is unusual in the context of the exercise of moral rights, and represents an interesting example in this connection.

Computer programs

Computer programs are protected as works, the exploitation rights being presumed, save contrary proof, to be ceded to the producer of the program (*i.e.* the natural or legal person who is responsible for the production of the work (art. 5)). The basic protection period is 60 years (art. 26).

Employee's works and commissioned works

The exploitation rights in employee's works and in commissioned works are presumed, subject to express contract to the contrary, to be ceded to the employer or commissioner (art. 59).

Performer's rights

The performer is granted exclusive rights of fixation and reproduction and (subject to remuneration right, see below) public communication of his performance, together with moral rights of attribution and integrity (art. 92).

Phonogram producer's rights

The phonogram producer is granted exclusive rights of reproduction, importation, distribution to the public and rental or other use of his phonogram, together with remuneration right (see below).

Phonogram performing right

Phonogram producers have the right to receive remuneration for the communication of phonograms to the public (with the general exceptions of art. 43). The wide definition of public communication in article 40 indicates that the remuneration right covers broadcasting, all forms of cabling, and public performance. Phonogram producers are obliged to share the remuneration 50/50 with the performers (art. 97). An unusual provision is contained in article 98: the remuneration payable under article 96 must not exceed 60 per cent. of the payments to the authors of the works contained in the phonograms.

Rental

Authors and phonogram producers have rental rights: see paragraph 20.31.

Convention membership

B(P), U(G), P, W.

Remedies and penalties

Extensive provisions concerning civil actions are contained in articles 109 to 118. Penal sanctions, with dispositions as to terms of imprisonment, are contained in articles 119 to 124.

[January 1994]

Yugoslavia

47.60 For a summary of the position as regards the constituent States of the former Yugoslavia, see paragraph 21.01. See also the entries in the Synopsis of Laws under Bosnia-Herzegovina (para. 23.90), Croatia (para. 27.35), Macedonia (para. 35.20), Montenegro (para. 37.00), Serbia (para. 42.35) and Slovenia (para. 42.68).

[January 1994]

49.00

Associated and other territories

Isle of Man: see paragraph 32.70.

[January 1994]

BIBLIOGRAPHY

Books, monographs and Articles

B Specific topics

Agnew, D.E., "Reform in the international protection of sound recordings: upsetting the delicate balance between authors, performers, and producers, or pragmatism in the age of digital piracy" [1992] *Ent. L.R.* 125 [8.04]

Banke L.M. and Shønning P., "New remuneration schemes in Denmark" *Copyright World* 1993, March, 33 [20.28]

Beard, J.L., "Casting call at Forest Lawn: the digital resurrection of deceased entertainers—a 21st Century challenge for intellectual property law" 41 *J. Copr. Soc'y*, 19 (1993) [3.24]

Beard, J.L., "Computer generated synthetic actors—a novel challenge for copyright law" *Copyright World* 1994, March, 24 [3.24]

Bently, L. and Sherman, B., "Cultures of copying: digital sampling and copyright law" [1992] *Ent. L.R.* 158 [4.14]

Berman, J., "The Audio Home Recording Act of 1991: a road to compromise" [1992] *Ent. L.R.* 64 [20.28]

Bertrand, A., "Performing rights societies: the price is right 'French-style', or the SACEM cases" [1992] *Ent. L.R.* 146 [7.38]

Boytha, G., "Intellectual property status of sound recordings" *IIC* 1993, 295 [6.01]

Bradshaw, D., "Fair dealing, and the Clockwork Orange case: a 'thieves' charter?" [1994] *Ent. L.R.* 7 [7.41]

Brown J., and Robert G., "The European Economic Area: how important is it?" [1992] *EIPR* 379 [7.54]

Brylawski, E.F., "Motion picture soundtrack music: a gap or gaff in copyright protection" 40 *J. Copr. Soc'y* 333 (1993) [45.90]

Chengsi Zheng, "The Chinese copyright system and the three relevant Conventions" *Copyright World* December 1992/January 1993, 33 [26.00]

Cornish, W., "Sound recordings and copyright" *IIC* 1993, 306 [6.01]

Curtis, N., "Satellite-delivered Pay TV services: the copyright issues relating to film" [1992] *Ent. L.R.* 71 [8.16]

Davies G. and Hung M., *Music and Video Private Copying* (Sweet & Maxwell, 1993) [20.28]

Dean, O.H., "Sound recordings in South Africa—the Cinderella of the copyright family" *Copyright World* 1993, October, 18 [42.90]

Dietz, A., "Protection of sound recordings in Central and Eastern Europe" [1993] *Ent. L.R.* 99 [24.70, 27.70, 31.90, 40.30, 41.00, 42.65]

Dreier, T., *Kabelweiterleitung und Urheberrecht—eine vergleichende Darstellung* (Beck'sche, 1991) [20.21]

Du Bois, R., "The legal aspects of sound sampling" *UNESCO Cop. Bull.* 1992, XXVI/2/7 [4.14]

Dworkin, G. and Sterling, J.A.L., "Phil Collins and the Term Directive" [1994] *EIPR* 187 [7.51]

Edelman, B., "Applicable legislation regarding exploitation of colourised U.S. films in France: the '*John Huston*' case" *IIC* 1992, 629 [7.15]

Fabiani, M., "Diffusione di trasmissioni televise in camere d'albergo e diritti di autore sulle opere telediffuse" *Il Diritto di Autore* 1992, 126 [7.25]

Fabiani, M., "La durata di protezione dei cartoni animati di Walt Disney" *Il Diritto di Autore* 1992, 575 [32.90]

Fine, F.L. "The impact of EEC Competition law on the music industry" [1992] *Ent. L.R.* 6 [7.38]

Gao Linghan, "Rules for the implementation of the Berne Convention in the People's Republic of China" *IIC* 1993, 475 [26.00]

Gendreau, Y. and MacKaay, E., *Canadian Legislation on Intellectual Property* (Carswell, 1993) [25.30]

Glick, M. and Page, M., "Copyright protection of video games in the United States" [1992] *EIPR*, 24 [4.26]

Goodenough, O.R., "Television via telephone lines: regulation and fibre optic revolution in the United States" [1992] *Ent. L.R.* 66 [8.16]

Goodenough, O.R., "The price of fame: the development of the right of publicity in the United States" [1992] *EIPR* 55 and 90 [7B.04]

Gringras, C., "Copyright in sound recordings in the United Kingdom" *Copyright World* 1994, March, 31 [4.14]

Harbottle, G., "Criminal remedies for copyright and performers' rights infringement under the Copyright, Designs and Patents Act 1988" [1994] *Ent. L.R.* 12 [45.70]

Karjala, D.S., "Recent United States and international developments in software protection" [1994] *EIPR* 13 and 58 [4.25]

Karnell, G., "The broadcasting of audiovisual works and moral rights" *Copyright World* December 1993/January 1994, 24 [4.69]

Keane, T.M., "The new Copyright Law in Cyprus" *Copyright World* 1994, February, 31 [27.50]

Kern, Ph., "The E.C. 'Common Position' on copyright applicable to satellite broadcasting and cable retransmission" [1993] *EIPR*, 276 [7.51]

Komen, E., "NAFTA's copyright magic show: retroactive protection for films does a disappearing act" *Copyright World* 1994, February, 44 [7.56]

Koumantos, G., "The new Greek Law on author's right and neighbouring rights" *RIDA* 159, 204 [30.60]

Logie, Ph., "The Dechavanne case: unauthorised sound sampling of a distinctive voice" [1993] *Ent. L.R.* 121 [4.14]

McDonald, B.W., "WIPO Symposium: debate intensifies over copyright issues raised by digital technology and information networks" *Copyright World* 1993, June, 20 [8.15]

Mallam, P., "Legal aspects of the globalisation of Pay TV" [1993] *Ent. L.R.* 43 [8.16]

Neumann, P. and Ehlers, M.R., "Denmark's new levy on blank audio and video tapes to compensate authors and creative artists for private copying" [1993] *Ent. L.R.* 25 [20.28]

Pisuke, H. and Ilja M.-E., "Copyright developments in the Baltic States" *Copyright World* 1993, July/August, 30 [34.90]

Pisuke H., "Estonia again on the world copyright map" *Copyright World* 1993, March, 24 [28.60]

Regnier, O., "Who framed Article 18? The protection of pre-1989 works in the U.S.A. under the Berne Convention" [1993] *EIPR* 400 [45.90]

Reinbothe, J., and von Lewinski, S., *The E.C. Directive on Rental and Lending Rights and on Piracy* (Sweet & Maxwell, 1993) [7.51]

Reinbothe, J. and von Lewinski, S., "The E.C. Rental Directive one year after its adoption: some selected issues" [1993] *Ent. L.R.* 169 [7.51]

Rinck, G.M., "The maturing U.S. law on copyright protection for computer programs" [1992] *EIPR* 351 [4.25]

Ricketson, S., *The Berne Convention for the protection of literary and artistic works: 1886–1986* (Queen Mary College/Kluwer, 1987) [42.80]

Rothnie, W.A., *Parallel Imports* (Sweet & Maxwell, 1993)

Rumphorst, W., "Protection of broadcasting organisations under the Rome Convention", *UNESCO Cop. Bull.* 1993, XXVII/2/10, and Opinion in [1992] *EIPR* 339 [7.46]

Sato, T. and Ohno, S., "Entertainment aspects of Japan's new Copyright Law" [1993] *Ent. L.R.* 89 [20.28]

Sherrard, B.G., "Performers' protection: the evolution of a complete offence" [1992] *Ent. L.R.* 57 [7B.20]

Silvestro, A., "Towards E.C. harmonisation of the term of protection of copyright and so-called 'related' rights" [1993] *Ent. L.R.* 73 [7.51]

Sodipo B., "Nigeria accedes to the Rome Convention: is Rome satisfactory for Nigerian performers?" [1994] *Ent. L.R.* 20 [38.50]

Stern, R.H., "The Game Genie case: copyright in derivative works versus users' rights" [1992] *Ent. L.R.* 104 [4.26]

Stone, R., "Copyright in the underlying works of motion picture films: solving distribution and exploitation difficulties through declaratory relief" [1993] *Ent. L.R.* 40 [45.70]

INDEX OF COUNTRIES AND TERRITORIES

References in the following list indicate amendments or additions to the Table A Addendum (covering membership of the Berne, U.C., Rome and Phonograms Conventions), List I (levels of protection, para. 20.22), List II (duration of protection, para. 20.25), Summary Chart (para. 20.51, as concerns Lists I and II), List III (private copying payments, para. 20.28), List IV (rental, para. 20.31), and the lists regarding performers' rights (paras. 7B.21-7B.23), resulting from new legislation as recorded in the Supplement. For details of amendments to the Summary Chart (including those regarding performances), see paragraph 20.51. The details of the changes will be found under the respective synopsis paragraph numbers as indicated.

21.20 **ALBANIA**
Table A Addendum

21.60 **ANGOLA**
List I, II, Chart CR/W
List V: delete asterisk

21.90 **ARGENTINA**
Table A Addendum

22.00 **ARMENIA**
List I, II, Chart CR/W

22.30 **AUSTRALIA**
Table A Addendum
List III Audio, Video

22.60 **AUSTRIA**
List IV PR, CR
Performers

22.70 **AZERBAIDJAN**
List I, II, Chart CR/W

22.95 **BAHRAIN**
List I, II, Chart CR/W
List V: delete asterisk

Index of Countries and Territories

23.45 **BELARUS**
List I, II, Chart CR/W

23.80 **BOLIVIA**
Table A Addendum
List I, II, Chart PR/W
List IV PR
Performers

23.90 **BOSNIA-HERZEGOVINA**
Table A Addendum
List I, II, Chart CR/W
Performers

24.70 **BULGARIA**
List II, Chart PR/W
List III Audio, Video
List IV PR, CR
Performers

25.30 **CANADA**
List IV PR

25.90 **CHILE**
List I, II, Chart PR/W
List IV PR
Performers

26.00 **CHINA**
Table A Addendum
List I, Chart PR/W, CR/W
List IV, PR, CR

27.35 **CROATIA**
Table A Addendum
List I, II, Chart CR/W
Performers

27.50 **CYPRUS**
Table A Addendum
List II, Chart PR/W
List IV CR

27.60 **CZECHOSLOVAKIA**
See paragraphs 27.70, 42.65.

Index of Countries and Territories

27.70 **CZECH REPUBLIC**
Table A Addendum
List I, II, Chart PR/W, CR/W
List III Audio, Video
List IV PR, CR
Performers

27.80 **DENMARK**
List III Audio, Video
List IV
Performers

28.50 **EL SALVADOR**
Table A Addendum
List II, Chart PR/W, CR/W
List IV PR, CR
Performers

28.60 **ESTONIA**
List I, II, Chart PR/W, CR/W
List III Audio, Video
List IV PR, CR
Performers

29.20 **FINLAND**
List I, II, Chart PR/W
List IV PR, CR
Performers

20.30 **FRANCE**
List III Audio, Video
List IV PR, CR

30.00 **GAMBIA**
Table A Addendum

30.10 **GEORGIA**
List I, II, Chart CR/W

30.50 **GREECE**
Table A Addendum
List I, II, Chart PR/W
List III Audio, Video
List IV PR, CR
Performers

Index of Countries and Territories

32.10 **ICELAND**
List II, Chart PR/W
List IV
Performers

32.70 **ISLE OF MAN**
Chart PR/W, CR/W
List IV PR, CR

32.90 **ITALY**
List III Audio, Video
List IV
Performers

33.10 **JAMAICA**
Table A Addendum
List I, PR/W, CR/W; List II CR/W
Chart PR/W, CR/W
List IV PR, CR
Performers

33.20 **JAPAN**
List III Audio, Video
Performers

33.30 **JORDAN**
List I, II, Chart CR/W
Performers

33.60 **KAZAKHSTAN**
Table A Addendum
List I, II, Chart CR/W

33.70 **KENYA**
Table A Addendum

33.75 **KIRGHIZIA**
List I, II, Chart CR/W

24.35 **LATVIA**
List I, II, Chart PR/W, CR/W
List IV PR, CR
Performers

34.90 **LITHUANIA**
List I, II, Chart CR/W

Index of Countries and Territories

35.20 **MACEDONIA**
Table A Addendum
List I, II, Chart CR/W
Performers

36.70 **MOLDOVA**
List I, II, Chart CR/W

36.80 **MONACO**
Correction The paragraph reference number is 36.80, not 38.00

37.00 **MONTENEGRO**
List I, II, Chart CR/W
Performers

37.40 **NAMIBIA**
Table A Addendum
List I, II, Chart PR/W, CR/W
List V delete asterisk

37.70 **NETHERLANDS**
Table A Addendum
List I, II, Chart PR/W
List III Audio, Video
Performers

38.50 **NIGERIA**
Table A Addendum
List III Audio, Video

38.90 **NORWAY**
Chart CR/W

41.10 **RUSSIAN FEDERATION**
Table A Addendum
List I, II, Chart PR/W, CR/W
List III Audio, Video
List IV PR, CR
Performers

41.60 **ST. LUCIA**
Table A Addendum

Index of Countries and Territories

41.80 **ST. VINCENT AND THE GRENADINES**
List I PR/W, CR/W; List II PR/W
Chart PR/W, CR/W
List IV PR
Performers

42.00 **SAN MARINO**
List II, Chart PR/W
Performers

42.35 **SERBIA**
List I, II, Chart CR/W
Performers

42.65 **SLOVAK REPUBLIC**
Table A Addendum
List I, II, Chart PR/W, CR/W
List III Audio, Video
List IV PR, CR
Performers

42.68 **SLOVENIA**
Table A Addendum
List I, II, Chart CR/W
Performers

43.00 **SPAIN**
List III Audio, Video

43.60 **SWEDEN**
Chart CR/W

43.70 **SWITZERLAND**
Table A Addendum
List I, II, Chart PR/W
List III Audio, Video
List IV PR, CR
Performers

43.90 **TADJIKISTAN**
Table A Addendum
List I, II, Chart CR/W

Index of Countries and Territories

- **44.00 TAIWAN**
  List II, Chart PR/W, CR/W
  List IV PR, CR

- **44.30 TOGO**
  List I, II, Chart PR/W
  Performers

- **45.00 TURKMENISTAN**
  List I, II, Chart CR/W

- **45.35 UKRAINE**
  List I, II, Chart C R/W

- **45.40 UNION OF SOVIET SOCIALIST REPUBLICS**
  See paragraph 21.01

- **45.60 UNITED ARAB EMIRATES**
  List I, II, Chart CR/W
  List V: delete asterisk

- **45.90 UNITED STATES OF AMERICA**
  List III Audio
  Performers

- **46.20 URUGUAY**
  Table A Addendum

- **46.30 UZBEKISTAN**
  List I, II, Chart CR/W

- **46.60 VENEZUELA**
  List I, II, Chart PR/W
  List IV PR, CR
  Performers

- **47.60 YUGOSLAVIA**
  See paragraph 21.01

GENERAL INDEX

Albania,
  Law of, synopsis, 21.20
Angola,
  Law of, synopsis, 21.60
Argentina,
  Law of, synopsis, 21.90
Armenia,
  Law of, synopsis, 22.00
Asian Pacific Economic Co-operation forum (APEC), 7.56
Audiovisual Works Registration Treaty 1988, 7.49
Australia,
  Law of, synopsis, 22.30
Austria,
  Law of, synopsis, 22.60
Azerbaidjan,
  Law of, synopsis, 22.70

Bahrain,
  Law of, synopsis, 22.95
Belarus,
  Law of, synopsis, 23.25
Belgium,
  Law of, synopsis, 23.30
Berne Convention,
  possible protocol, 7.53
  membership of, 7.51, 20.11
  See also Table of International Treaties, Conventions and Agreements
Bhutan, 20.34
Blank tape payments,
  national law provisions, 20.28
Bogsch theory, 7.51

Bolivia,
  Law of, synopsis, 23.80
Bosnia-Herzegovina,
  Law of, synopsis, 23.90
Brazil,
  Law of, synopsis, 24.10
Broadcasting,
  direct, by satellite (DBS), 7.26
Broadcasting organisations,
  protection of, under Rome Convention, 7.46
Brunei Darussalam, 20.34
Bulgaria,
  Law of, synopsis, 24.70

Cable retransmission,
  EEC Directive on, 7.51B
Canada,
  Law of, synopsis, 25.30
Chile,
  Law of, synopsis, 25.90
China,
  Law of, synopsis, 26.00
Colombia,
  Law of, synopsis, 26.50
Colourisation of films, 7.15
Computer,
  storage in, copying by, 4.24
Computer program,
  infringement, 4.25
Computer-simulated actors, 3.24
Counterfeit and pirated goods,
  circulation of, 7.42
Croatia,
  Law of, synopsis, 27.35

Cyprus,
  Law of, synopsis, 27.50
Czechoslovakia,
  Law of, synopsis, 27.60
Czech Republic,
  Law of, synopsis, 27.70

Database,
  Proposed EEC Directive, 7.51D
DBS (direct broadcasting by satellite), *see under* **Broadcasting**
Denmark,
  Law of, synopsis, 27.80
Descramblers, unauthorised making of, 7.42

Ecuador,
  Law of, synopsis, 28.30
Egypt,
  Law of, synopsis, 28.40
El Salvador,
  Law of, synopsis, 28.50
Estonia,
  Law of, synopsis, 28.60
European Economic Area (EEA),
  Agreement, 7.54
  See also **Table of European Materials**
European Economic Community (EEC)
  Council Directives, 7.51
    rental and lending rights, and related rights, 7.51A, 20.31
    satellite broadcasting and cable retransmission, 7.51B
    term of protection, 7.51C
  Working programme, 7.51D
  See also **Table of European Materials**
European Free Trade Association (EFTA), 7.54

European Union, 7.51

'**Fair dealing**', 7.41
Finland,
  Law of, synopsis, 29.20
Forgery,
  videotapes, of, 7.42
France,
  Law of, synopsis, 29.30

Gambia,
  Law of, synopsis, 30.00
GATT-TRIPs Agreement, 7.52
  See also **Table of International Treaties, Conventions and Agreements** (1993)
Georgia,
  Law of, synopsis, 30.10
Germany,
  Law of, synopsis, 30.20
Greece,
  Law of, synopsis, 30.50

Honduras,
  Law of, synopsis, 31.70
Hungary,
  Law of, synopsis, 31.90

Iceland,
  Law of, synopsis, 32.10
Imports, parallel, 4.45
  Australia, under law of, 22.30
  Norway, under law of, 38.90
  United States, under law of, 45.90
India,
  Law of, synopsis, 32.20
Ireland,
  Law of, synopsis, 32.60
Isle of Man,
  Law of, synopsis, 32.70

Italy,
  Law of, synopsis, 32.90

Jamaica,
  Law of, synopsis, 33.10
Japan,
  Law of, synopsis, 33.20
Jordan,
  Law of, synopsis, 7.05, 33.30

Kazakhstan,
  Law of, synopsis, 33.60
Kenya,
  Law of, synopsis, 33.70
Kirghizia,
  Law of, synopsis, 33.75

Latvia,
  Law of, synopsis, 34.35
Lending,
  EEC Directive on, 7.51A
Lithuania,
  Law of, synopsis, 34.90
Luxembourg,
  Law of, synopsis, 35.00

Macedonia,
  Law of, synopsis, 35.20
Malta,
  Law of, synopsis, 36.00
Mexico
  Law of, synopsis, 36.50
Misappropriation, tort of, 7.42
Moldova,
  Law of, synopsis, 36.70
Monaco,
  Main text, Index of Countries and Territories and General Index (*correction*), 36.80
Montenegro
  Law of, synopsis, 37.00

Moral rights,
  Audiovisual works, 4.69
  national law provisions, France, 7.15
  E.C. discussions, 7.51D

Namibia,
  Law of, synopsis, 37.40
National treatment,
  under E.C. law, 7.38
Neighbouring rights, 7.50, 7.51
Netherlands,
  Law of, synopsis, 37.70
Niger,
  Law of, synopsis, 38.40
Nigeria
  Law of, synopsis, 38.50
North American Free Trade Agreement, 1992, (NAFTA), 7.55, 20.31
  See also **Table of International Treaties, Conventions and Agreements**
Norway,
  Law of, synopsis, 38.90

Pay TV, 8.16
Performance, public,
  hotel rooms, 7.25
Performers,
  possible Instrument for protection of, 7.53
  recordings, remuneration for use of, *see* **Record Performing Right**
  rights of,
    duration of protection, 7B.22
    levels of protection, 7B.21
    non-protecting countries, 7B.24
    private copying, 7B.23
    regional protection, 7C.01–7C.07
    rental, 7B.23

Phonograms Convention,
  membership of, 20.11
  See also **Table of International Treaties, Conventions and Agreements**
Poland,
  Law of, synopsis, 40.30
Portugal,
  Law of, synopsis, 40.40
Private copying,
  E.C. consultation document, 7.51D
  performers' rights, 7B.23
  remuneration for, summary of national laws, 20.28
Protection,
  duration of rights, 7.09
    under national laws, 20.25
  levels of,
    under national laws, 20.22–20.23
  term of,
    EEC Directive on, 7.51C
Producer, cinematographic,
  regional protection, 7C.01-7C.08
  See also under Synopsis of law (paras 21.00 et seq.) under respective countries
Producer, phonographic,
  possible Instrument for protection of, 7.53
  regional protection, 7C.01–7C.07
  See also under Synopsis of laws (paras 21.00 et seq.) under respective countries
Publicity, right of, 7B.04

Record performing right, 7A.05
  Rome Convention (Art. 12), 7.42
Recording machine payments, 20.28

Rental,
  EEC Directive on, 7.51A
  national laws, 20.31
  performers' rights, 7B.23
Romania,
  Law of, synopsis, 41.00
Rome Convention,
  broadcasting/public communication of phonograms (Art. 12), 7.46, 7A.10
  membership of, 7B.07, 20.11
  See also **Table of International Treaties, Conventions and Agreements**
Russian Federation,
  Law of, synopsis, 41.10

St. Lucia,
  Law of, synopsis, 41.60
St. Vincent and the Grenadines,
  Law of, synopsis, 41.80
Sampling, 4.14
San Marino,
  Law of, synopsis, 42.00
Satellite broadcasting,
  EEC Directive on, 7.51B
Satellites Convention,
  membership of, 20.12
  See also **Table of International Treaties, Conventions and Agreements**
Saudi Arabia,
  Law of, synopsis, 42.20
Screen displays, 4.26
Serbia,
  Law of, synopsis, 42.35
Seychelles,
  Law of, synopsis, 42.40
Slovak Republic,
  Law of, synopsis, 42.65
Slovenia,
  Law of, synopsis, 42.68

Sound recording,
  protection of, 8.04
  history of, 6.01
South Africa,
  Law of, synopsis, 42.90
Spain,
  Law of, synopsis, 43.00
Sweden,
  Law of, synopsis, 43.60
Switzerland,
  Law of, synopsis, 43.70

Tadjikistan,
  Law of, synopsis, 43.90
Taiwan,
  Law of, synopsis, 44.00
Television via telephone, 8.16
Thailand,
  Law of, synopsis, 44.20
Togo,
  Law of, synopsis, 44.30
TRIPs Agrement: *see* **GATT-TRIPs Agreement**
Tunisia,
  Law of, synopsis, 44.80
Turkmenistan,
  Law of, synopsis, 45.00

Universal Copyright Convention,
  membership of, 20.11
  See also **Table of International Treaties, Conventions and Agreements**
Ukraine,
  Law of, synopsis, 45.35

Union of Soviet Socialist Republics, 21.01, 45.40
United Arab Emirates,
  Law of, synopsis, 45.60
United Kingdom,
  Law of, synopsis, 45.70
United States of America,
  Law of, synopsis, 45.90
Uruguay,
  Law of, synopsis, 46.20
Uzbekistan,
  Law of, synopsis, 46.30

Venezuela,
  Law of, synopsis, 46.60
Videogames, 4.26
Video tapes,
  forgery of, 7.42

WIPO Convention,
  membership of, 20.11
  see also **Table of International Treaties, Conventions and Agreements**
WIPO Possible Protocol to Berne Convention, 7.53
WIPO Possible Instrument on the Protection of Performers and Producers of Phonograms, 7.52

Yugoslavia,
  21.01, 47.60